teach®
yourself

spanish phrasebook
rosa maría martín

For over sixty years, more than
40 million people have learnt over
750 subjects the **teach yourself**
way, with impressive results.

be where you want to be
with **teach yourself**

For UK order enquiries: please contact Bookpoint Ltd, 130 Milton Park, Abingdon, Oxon OX14 4SB. Telephone: +44 (0)1235 827720. Fax: +44 (0)1235 400454. Lines are open 09.00–18.00, Monday to Saturday, with a 24-hour message answering service. Details about our titles and how to order are available at www.teachyourself.co.uk

For USA order enquiries: please contact McGraw-Hill Customer Services, PO Box 545, Blacklick, OH 43004-0545, USA. Telephone: 1-800-722-4726. Fax: 1-614-755-5645.

For Canada order enquiries: please contact McGraw-Hill Ryerson Ltd, 300 Water St, Whitby, Ontario L1N 9B6, Canada. Telephone: 905 430 5000. Fax: 905 430 5020.

Long renowned as the authoritative source for self-guided learning – with more than 30 million copies sold worldwide – **the teach yourself** series includes over 300 titles in the fields of languages, crafts, hobbies, business, computing and education.

British Library Cataloguing in Publication Data: a catalogue record for this title is available from the British Library.

Library of Congress Catalog Card Number: on file.

First published in UK 2004 by Hodder Arnold, 338 Euston Road, London, NW1 3BH.

First published in US 2005 by Contemporary Books, a division of the McGraw-Hill Companies, 1 Prudential Plaza, 130 East Randolph Street, Chicago, IL 60601 USA.

This edition published 2004.

The **teach yourself** name is a registered trade mark of Hodder Headline Ltd.

Author: Rosa María Martín

Text and illustrations © Hodder & Stoughton Educational 2004

Printed and bound by Graphycems, Spain.

Impression number 10 9 8 7 6 5 4 3 2 1

Year 2010 2009 2008 2007 2006 2005 2004

CONTENTS

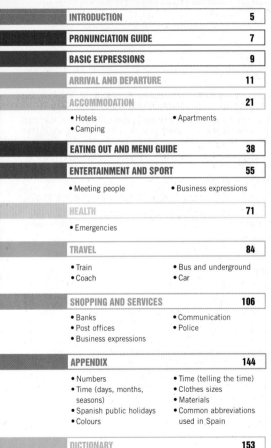

INTRODUCTION

This *Teach Yourself Spanish Phrasebook* is an essential accessory
for visitors to Spain and other Spanish-speaking countries, of
whatever age and for whatever purpose. It provides a thorough
survival guide with useful phrases in authentic but simple modern
Spanish, in clearly defined logical sections for quick and easy
reference.

Features include:

- Up-to-date information sections about modern
  Spanish life.

- A full alphabetical wordlist for quick reference.

- A simple, consistent and effective pronunciation guide.

- Key root sentences and phrases suitable for a variety of
  situations through substitution of appropriate vocabulary.

- Simple and effective questions to obtain short answers, avoiding
  confusion.

- Suggestions for some of the answers you might hear in response
  to your questions.

- A special general information reference section making this
  much more than just a phrasebook.

- A section of basic expressions suitable for many situations.

In Spanish there is a difference between 'you' used formally (*usted*) and informally (*tú*). Phrases and expressions employing one or the other are clearly indicated, and where both are suitable, both options are given.

Generally, Spanish nouns end in **o** for masculine nouns (*el*) and in **a** for feminine nouns (*la*). Where this is not the case, the wordlist section indicates clearly by the symbol **m** or **f** after the word in question.

You can prepare yourself before your visit by practising a number of the more common basic expressions and becoming familiar with Spanish pronunciation patterns outlined in the book, although it can be equally effective when used 'on site'.

¡Buen viaje!

PRONUNCIATION GUIDE

Spanish pronunciation is very straightforward: everything is pronounced, and letters are always pronounced the same way. The following guide is used to indicate pronunciation that differs from English. In this phrasebook the stressed syllable in each word is indicated in bold type.

SYMBOL		SPANISH WORD		ENGLISH WORD
a	*as in*	padre	*compare with*	pat
air		reserva		fair
e		tengo		tent
ee		vida		me
eh		doble		bled

I	hay	buy
o	quiero	low
oo	uva	soon
y	habitación	yes
b	baño	see below
v	lavabo	see below
ch	plancha	church
g	gato	get
h	jabón	see below
k	cama	cat
r	querer	see below
s	estrella	glass
th	cerca	thick

- **b** and **v** sound the same in Spanish. At the beginning of a word or syllable, both are pronounced like English **b** as in 'big'. In the middle of a word, it is a softer sound.

- **g** is sometimes and **j** is always pronounced at the back of the throat, like the **ch** in Scottish lo**ch**. The symbol **h** is used when this occurs. (Do not confuse this with **eh**. Where the **h** symbol coincides with the **e** symbol, they are separated with a hyphen.)

- **r** is always strongly pronounced: it is rolled like a Scottish **r**.

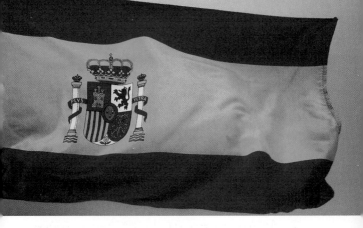

BASIC EXPRESSIONS

yes	sí
	see
no	no
	no
please	por favor
	por fabbor
thank you	gracias
	grath-yas
that's enough	basta
	basta
I don't know	no sé
	no seh

I'm sorry/excuse me	perdón *pairdon*
I can't...	no puedo *no pweddo*
I'm (very) sorry	lo siento (mucho) *lo see-yento (moocho)*
excuse me (to get attention)	oiga, por favor *oyga, por fabbor*
Mr/Sir	Señor *senyor*
Mrs/Madam	Señora *senyora*
Miss	Señorita *senyoreeta*
my name is (Smith)	mi nombre es (Smith) *mee nombreh es (Smith)*
just a moment	un momento *oon momento*
I (don't) like it	(no) me gusta *(no) meh goosta*
I (don't) want it	(no) lo quiero *(no) lo kee-yerro*
How much is it?	¿Cuánto es? *kwanto es?*
Do you accept credit cards?	¿Aceptan tarjetas de crédito? *atheptan tarhetas deh kreditto?*
I don't understand	No comprendo *no komprendo*
Do you speak English?	¿Habla inglés? *abla ingles?*

ARRIVAL AND DEPARTURE

ENTERING THE COUNTRY

As a member of the European Union, Spain has the same border regulations as other European countries. If arriving by air or boat you will be asked to show your passport. When arriving by road, all borders are now open and you will not normally be stopped. For some non-EU visitors, visas are sometimes required. Check with the Spanish consulate before you travel.

I'm here...	Vengo...
	bengo...
...on holiday	...de vacaciones
	deh bakathyon-es
...on business	...de negocios
	deh negoth-yos

...to visit some friends	...a visitar a unos amigos *a beeseetar a oonos ameegos*
...for two weeks	...para dos semanas *para dos semanas*
...for a month	...para un mes *para oon mes*
I'll be at this address	Estaré en esta dirección *estareh en esta dirrekth-yon*
We're passing through	Vamos de paso *bamos deh paso*
I've lost my passport	He perdido mi pasaporte *eh pairdeedo mee pasaporteh*

For some non-EU visitors, visas are sometimes required. Check with the Spanish consulate before you travel.

LUGGAGE

Where are the trolleys?	¿Dónde están los carros/carritos? *dondeh estan los karros/karreetos?*
I can't find...	No encuentro... *no enkwentro...*
...my bag	...mi bolsa *mee bolsa*
...my luggage	...mi equipaje *mee ekeepaheh*
...my suitcase	...mi maleta *mee maletta*
Could you carry my luggage?	¿Puede llevarme el equipaje? *pwedeh yebbarmeh el ekeepaheh?*
It's this one	Es esto *es esto*
How much do I owe you?	¿Cuánto le debo? *kwanto le debbo?*

AT THE INFORMATION DESK

Where is...?	¿Dónde está...?
	dondeh esta...?
...the taxi rank	...la parada de taxis
	la parada deh taxees
...the bus to the city	...el autobús a la ciudad
	el owtoboos a la theeoodad
...the train	...el tren
	el tren
...the underground	...el metro
	el metro
...the left luggage office	...la consigna
	la konseegna
Where can I...?	¿Dónde puedo...?
	dondeh pwedo...?
...buy a ticket	...comprar un billete
	komprar oon beeyeteh
...change money	...cambiar dinero
	kamb-yar dinerro
...hire a car	...alquilar un coche
	alkeelar oon kocheh
...make a phone call	...llamar por teléfono
	yamar por telefono
Could you give me...?	¿Puede darme...?
	pwedeh darmeh...?
...a bus timetable	...un horario de autobuses
	oon orareeo deh owtobooses
...a brochure of (the town)	...un folleto de (la ciudad)
	oon foyetto deh (la theeoodad)
...a list of hotels	...una lista de hoteles
	oona leesta deh otel-es
...a train timetable	...un horario de trenes
	oon orareeo deh tren-es

Could you find me a... hotel?	¿Puede buscarme un hotel...? *pwedeh booskarmeh oon otel...?*
...luxury	...de lujo *deh loo-ho*
...three star	...de tres estrellas *deh tres estreyas*
...economic/cheap	...barato *barato*

ASKING THE WAY

Excuse me	Oiga, por favor *oyga, por fabbor*
How do I get...?	¿Para ir...? *para eer...?*
...to Benidorm	...a Benidorm *a beneedorm*
...to the Hotel (Sol)	...al hotel (Sol) *al otel (sol)*
...to the beach	...a la playa *a la plI-a*
...to the airport	...al aeropuerto *al aeropwairto*
How many kilometres to (Madrid)?	¿A cuántos kilómetros está (Madrid)? *a kwantos keelometros esta (madreed)?*
Do you have a map/a plan?	¿Tiene un mapa/un plano? *tee-yenneh oon mapa/oon plano?*
Where are the toilets/the shops?	¿Dónde están los servicios/ las tiendas? *dondeh estan los sairbeeth-yos/las tee-yendas?*

Is it a long way away/nearby?	¿Está lejos/cerca? *esta leh-hos/thairka?*
Do I have to take the bus/ the underground?	¿Tengo que tomar el autobús/el metro? *tengo keh tomar el owtoboos/el metro?*
Can you walk there?	¿Se puede ir a pie? *seh pwedeh eer a pee-yeh?*
Can you go with me?	¿Puede acompañarme? *pwedeh akompanyarmeh?*
Where is...?	¿Dónde está...? *dondeh esta...?*
...the station	...la estación *la estathyon*
...the underground station	...el metro *el metro*
...the train for the airport	...el tren para el aeropuerto *el tren para el aeropwairto*
...the taxi rank	...la parada de taxis *la parada deh taxees*
...the motorway to (Bilbao)	...la autopista a (Bilbao) *la owtopeesta a (beelbao)*
...the main road/dual carriageway to (Salamanca)	...la autovía a (Salamanca) *la owtobeea a (Salamanka)*
...the (Madrid) road	...la carretera de (Madrid) *la kareterra deh (madreed)*
...the police station	...la comisaría *la komeesareea*
...the tourist office	...la oficina de turismo *la ofeetheena deh tooreesmo*
...the town centre	...el centro *el thentro*

Where is there...?	¿Dónde hay...? *dondeh I...?*
...a bank	...un banco *oon banko*
...a post office	...una oficina de correos ***oo**na ofee**thee**na deh korr**ay**-os*
...a car park	...un parking *oon parkeeng*
...a supermarket	...un supermercado *oon sooper-mairka**d**o*
...a telephone	...un teléfono *oon tele**f**ono*

You may hear:

la primera (calle) *la pre**e**mera (ka-yeh)*	the first (street)
la segunda *la seg**oo**nda*	the second
la tercera *la tair**th**era*	the third
a la derecha *a la derecha*	on the right
a la izquierda *a la eethkee-y**ai**rda*	on the left
todo recto *to**d**o rekto*	straight on
allí *ay**ee**.*	there
aquí (mismo) *akee (meesmo)*	(just) here
en el semáforo *en el sem**a**foro*	at the traffic lights

al final de la calle
al feenal deh la ka-yeh

at the end of the street

en la esquina
en la eskeena

on/at the corner

a (quince) kilómetros
a (keentheh) keelometros

(15) kms away

a (cinco) minutos
a (theenko) meenootos

(5) minutes away

tome el desvío
tomeh el desbeeo

take the diversion

no está lejos
no esta le-hos

it's not far

está cerca de...
esta thairka deh...

it's near...

TAXI

- Taxi fares vary from town to town. Taxis for hire show a **libre** sign and a green light.

- There is a basic charge plus a meter which should be visible to passengers. Extra charges may be made at night or for carrying extra luggage. You are advised to ask for a price if making a long journey.

- Tipping of between 5 and 10% is normal.

Taxi!	¡Taxi! *taxee!*
Could you take me...?	Por favor, lléveme... *por fabbor, yebbemeh...*
...here (when indicating an address)	aquí *akee*
...to this address	...a esta dirección *a esta dirrekth-yon*

Taxi fares vary from town to town. Taxis for hire show a *libre* sign and a green light.

...to the airport	...al aeropuerto *al aeropwairto*
...to the hotel (Sol)	...al hotel (Sol) *al otel (sol)*
How much is it to the city/ the airport?	¿Cuánto es hasta la ciudad/ el aeropuerto? *kwanto es asta la theeoodad/el aeropwairto?*
Could you stop here, please?	Pare aquí, por favor *pareh akee, por fabbor*
Could you...?	¿Puede...? *pwedeh...?*
...wait for me	...esperarme *esperarmeh*
...help me with my cases	...ayudarme con las maletas *ayoodarmeh kon las malettas*

- For directions see page 16.

CAR HIRE

- Most of the major car-hire companies are to be found at airports and in the main towns and cities, and brochures are available in English stating conditions and prices. Good deals for car hire can also be made through the Internet before you travel. You must be at least twenty-one to hire a car in Spain.

I've hired a car...	he alquilado un coche... *eh alkeelado oon kocheh...*
my name is...	mi nombre es... *mee nombreh es...*
I'd like to hire a small/big car	Quiero alquilar un coche pequeño/grande *keeyerro alkeelar oon kocheh pekenyo/grandeh*

For today/one week	Para hoy/una semana *para oy/oona semana*
How much is it daily/per kilometre?	¿Cuánto es por día/por kilómetro? *kwanto es por deea/por keelometro?*
Is insurance/mileage included?	¿Está incluido el seguro/ el kilometraje? *esta eenklooeedo el segooro/ el keelometraheh?*
I'd like comprehensive insurance	Quiero seguro a todo riesgo *kee-yerro segooro a todo ree-esgo*
Can I leave it in (Madrid)?	¿Puedo dejarlo en (Madrid)? *pwedo deh-harlo en (madreed)?*
Do you want my driving licence?	¿Quiere mi permiso de conducir? *kee-yerreh mee pairmeeso deh kondootheer?*

AT THE AIRPORT

Is there a flight to (Alicante)?	¿Hay un vuelo para (Alicante)? *I oon bwelo para (aleekanteh)?*
A ticket for (London), please	Un billete para (Londres), por favor *oon beeyeteh para (londres), por fabbor*
Do I have to make a connection?	¿Hay que hacer conexión? *I keh athair konex-yon?*
When do I have to check in?	¿Cuándo debo presentarme? *kwando debbo presentarmeh?*

You must be at least twenty-one to hire a car in Spain.

I want to...my flight	Quiero...mi vuelo *kee-yerro...mee bwelo*
...confirm	...confirmar *konfeermar*
...cancel	...cancelar *kanthelar*
...change	...cambiar *kamb-yar*
Where is...?	¿Dónde está...? *dondeh esta...?*
...the (Iberia) counter	...el mostrador (de Iberia) *el mostrador (deh eebereea)*
...the duty free shop	...la tienda libre de impuestos *la tee-yenda leebreh deh eempwestos*
Is it delayed?	¿Lleva retraso? *yebba retrasso?*
How much is it delayed?	¿Cuánto retraso hay? *kwanto retrasso I?*
I've missed my plane	He perdido mi avión *eh pairdeedo mee ab-yon*

ACCOMMODATION

HOTELS

• **H** (*Hotel*) followed by 1 to 5 stars. There are also some hotels categorised as *gran lujo* (great luxury) at the top end of the 5-star category.

Aparthotel is a combination of hotel and self-catering apartment. H (*Hostal*) and P (*Pensión*) from 1 to 3 stars. These offer more basic, cheaper accommodation and no meals. You may also see *Hostal Residencia* or *Casa de huéspedes* (Guest house).

A *Parador* is a state-owned luxury hotel, usually housed in a restored historic building in an area of outstanding natural beauty. Suitable as an overnight break for road travellers. Also well-known as excellent restaurants.

When registering you will be asked to show your passport at the desk and to complete a form.

- Other types of accommodation:
  - **F** (*Fonda*): cheap and basic
  - *Casa* + name of the owner or *Casa de huéspedes*: guest house
  - *Camas* (beds) or *Habitaciones* (rooms) usually found in private houses
  - *Albergue Juvenil*: youth hostel.
- A list of accommodation facilities can normally be found in the local tourist office. Employees may even help to reserve a place for you. In the high season it is advisable to book in advance.

- Nightly prices (per room and not per person) should be clearly displayed on the back of the door of your room. These are inclusive of tax (*IVA Incluido*).
  Breakfast is not always included in the price. **NOTE**: breakfast is 'Continental' but 'English Breakfast' may be available in some holiday resorts.

- When registering you will be asked to show your passport at the desk and to complete a form.

- All hotels and campsites are required by law to keep and produce complaints forms (*Hojas de Reclamaciones*) on request.

- You can ask for an extra bed in a double room. This will cost you a percentage of the price of the room.

- Full board (*Pensión Completa*) is usually more economical than taking your meals separately.

- Electrical appliances function with two-pin plugs. These require a special adaptor which you can purchase in Britain. Voltages are 220V.

Have you any rooms free?	¿Hay habitaciones libres? *I abeetath-yones leebres?*
I have a reservation	Tengo una reserva *tengo oona resairba*
I would like to make a reservation	Quiero hacer una reserva *kee-yerro athair oona resairba*
My name is...	Mi nombre es... *mee nombreh es*
Is there another hotel nearby?	¿Hay otro hotel cerca? *I otro otel thairka?*
I would like two rooms	Quiero dos habitaciones *kee-yerro dos abeetath-yones*
I would like a single/double room	Quiero una habitación individual/doble *kee-yerro oona abeetath-yon indibeedwal/dobbleh*
I would like a room...	Quiero una habitación... *kee-yerro oona abeetath-yon...*
...with a double bed	...con una cama doble *kon oona kama dobbleh*
...with two beds	...con dos camas *kon dos kamas*
...for three people	...para tres personas *parra tres pairsonas*
...with a cot	...con una cuna *kon oona koona*
...with a bath	...con baño *kon banyo*
...with a shower	...con ducha *kon doocha*
It's for...	Es para... *es para...*

Electrical appliances function with two-pin plugs. These require a special adaptor which you can purchase in Britain. Voltages are 220V.

...one night

...una noche
oona nocheh

...two nights

...dos noches
dos noch-es

...one week

...una semana
oona semana

...a fortnight

...quince días
kintheh deeas

How much is it?

¿Cuánto es?
kwanto es?

Can you write it down?

¿Puede escribirlo?
pwedeh eskreebeerlo?

Is there a supplementary
charge for another bed?

¿Hay suplemento por otra cama?
I sooplemento por otra kama?

Does the child pay?

¿El niño paga?
el neenyo paga?

He/she is...

Tiene...
tee-yeneh...

...six months old

...seis meses
seyes mes-es

...one year old

...un año
oon anyo

...five years old

...cinco años
theenko anyos

Can I have the bill please?

¿La cuenta por favor?
la kwenta por fabbor?

Do you accept credit cards?

¿Aceptan tarjetas de crédito?
atheptan tarhetas deh kreditto?

Can I see the room?

¿Puedo ver la habitación?
pwedo bair la abeetath-yon?

I will (won't) take it

(No) la tomo
(no) la tomo

It's...	Es... *es...*
...very expensive	...muy cara *mwee kara*
...too small	...demasiado pequeña *demas-yado pekenya*
...dark	...oscura *oskoora*
I would like another room	Quiero otra habitación *kee-yerro otra abeetath-yon*
Could you take my luggage up?	¿Puede subir el equipaje? *pwedeh soobeer el ekeepaheh?*
Is breakfast included?	¿Está incluido el desayuno? *esta eenklooeedo el desayoono?*
I'd like...	Quiero... *kee-yerro*
...breakfast only	...desayuno solo *desayoono solo*
...half board	...media pensión *med-ya pens-yon*
...full board	...pensión completa *pens-yon kompletta*
What time is...?	¿A qué hora es...? *a keh ora es...?*
...breakfast	...el desayuno *el desayoono*
...lunch	...la comida *la komeeda*
...dinner	...la cena *la thenna*

Could you bring breakfast to my room?	¿Puede traer el desayuno a mi habitación? *pwedeh tryair el desayoono a mee abeetathyon?*
Could you call me...?	¿Puede llamarme...? *pwedeh yamarmeh...?*
...for breakfast	...para el desayuno *para el desayoono*
...at seven o'clock	...a las siete *a las see-yetteh*
Can I have the key (for number 10), please?	Por favor, ¿la llave (de la número 10)? *por fabbor, la yabbeh (deh la noomero dee-eth)?*
Is there...?	¿Hay...? *I...?*
...air conditioning	...aire acondicionado *I-reh akondeeth-yonado*
...a lift	...ascensor *asthensor*
...a safe	...caja fuerte *kaha fwairteh*
Could you give me...?	¿Puede darme...? *pwedeh darmeh...?*
...an ashtray	...un cenicero *oon theneethero*
...another blanket	...otra manta *otra manta*
...a clothes hanger	...una percha *oona paircha*
...another pillow	...otra almohada *otra almo-ada*
...some soap	...jabón *habbon*

...another towel	...otra toalla *otra to-alya*
Could you...?	¿Puede...? *pwedeh...?*
...put this in the safe	...poner esto en la caja fuerte *ponair esto en la kaha fwairteh*
...call a taxi	...llamar un taxi *yammar oon taxee*
...bring down my luggage	...bajar el equipaje *bahar el ekeepaheh*
...get the bill ready (for tomorrow)	...preparar la cuenta (para mañana) *preparar la kwenta (para manyana)*
Are there any messages for me?	¿Hay recados para mí? *I rekados para mee?*
The bill is wrong	la cuenta está equivocada *la kwenta esta ekeebocada*
Excuse me but there's a mistake	Perdone, hay un error *pairdoneh I oon error*
It's wrong	Está mal *esta mal*

CAMPING

You may see:

Camping	camp site
Bungalows	holiday cabins
Caravanas	caravans
Cabinas	large caravans
1, 2, 3 categoría	1st, 2nd and 3rd class
De lujo	luxury

- It is advisable to book in advance at some of the more popular campsites in high season to avoid disappointment. You can find details of many Spanish campsites on the Internet (try www.spaintour.com). Write or phone direct to the site or contact the Spanish Camping Federation for more information at Federación Española de Empresarios de Campings, General Oráa 52-2 d, 28006 Madrid. Telephone ++34 91 562 9994. You can buy useful camping guides from bookshops and tourist offices with all the information you will need. If you intend to camp out of season, check which campsites are open. For many, the season runs from May to September. Some campsites hire out tents for use on the same site. Campsite rates vary depending on the quantity and quality of their services.

- When you arrive, reception will take information from your passport for their records.

- Children under sixteen must be accompanied by adults and children under eleven years old usually pay less.

- If you are thinking of camping outside established campsites or on private land, check beforehand with the authorities or the owners whether this is allowed. If you are allowed, there are often regulations regarding numbers of people, numbers of tents, number of days spent in one place, etc.

  You are not permitted to camp:

  - in dangerous or potentially dangerous places such as river banks or areas prone to flooding
  - on land owned or used by the military or by industry
  - within 150 metres of the main water supply for a town or village

It is advisable to book in advance at some of the more popular campsites in high season to avoid disappointment.

- within city limits
- on the side of the road
- within a kilometre of an existing campsite.

I have a reservation	Tengo una reserva *tengo oona resairba*
Could I see the camp site?	¿Puedo ver el camping? *pwedo bair el kamping?*
Have you spaces free?	¿Tiene plazas libres? *tee-yenneh plathas leebres?*
Could you write it down/ give me a leaflet with the prices?	¿Puede escribirlo/darme un folleto con los precios? *pwedeh eskreebeerlo/darmeh oon foyetto kon los preth-yos?*
I have...	Tengo... *tengo...*
...a small/big tent	...una tienda pequeña/grande *oona tee-yenda pekenya/grandeh*
...a caravan	...una caravana *oona karabana*
...a car	...un coche *oon kocheh*
How much is it...?	¿Cuánto es...? *kwanto es...?*
...per person	...por persona *por pairsona*
...for a child	...por un niño *por oon neenyo*
...per day	...por día *por deea*
...for the tent	...por la tienda *por la tee-yenda*

...for the car	...por el coche
	por el kocheh
It's for...	Es para...
	es para...
...two adults	...dos adultos
	dos adooltos
...and a child	...y un niño
	ee oon neenyo
...two nights	...dos noches
	dos noch-es
I prefer to be...	Prefiero estar...
	pref-yerro estar...
...in the shade	...en la sombra
	en la sombra
...near the beach	...cerca de la playa
	thairka deh la plI-a
...a long way from the road	...lejos de la carretera
	leh-hos deh la kareterra
Do you rent/have...?	¿Alquilan/tiene...?
	alkeelan/tee-yeneh...?
...tents	...tiendas
	tee-yendas
...caravans	...caravanas
	karabanas
...cabins	...cabinas
	kabeenas
...camping equipment	...material de camping
	matereeal deh kampeeng
...a refrigerator	...un frigorífico
	oon freegoreefiko
...a light	...un farol
	oon farol

...a torch	...una linterna *oona leentairna*
...mattresses	...colchonetas *kolchonettas*
...a broom	...una escoba *oona eskoba*
...a bottle of gas	...una botella de gas *oona botelya deh gas*
...a frying pan	...una sartén *oona sarten*

• For other items, see the **Dictionary**.

Does the campsite close at night?	¿Cierran el camping por la noche? *thee-yerran el kampeeng por la nocheh?*
At what time?	¿A qué hora? *a keh ora?*
Is/are there...?	¿Hay...? *I...?*
...a doctor	...médico *medikko*
...electricity	...conexión eléctrica *konex-yon elektreeka*
...a first aid box	...botiquín *boteekeen*
...sockets in the washblocks	...enchufes en los lavabos *enchoof-es en los lababos*
...ice	...hielo *yelo*
Where is/are...?	¿Dónde está/están...? *dondeh esta/estan...?*
...the ironing room	...la sala de plancha *la salla deh plancha*

...the rubbish bins	...los cubos de basura *los koobos deh basoora*
...the (hot water) showers	...las duchas (de agua caliente) *las doochas (deh agwa kal-yenteh)*
...the toilets	...los servicios *los sairbeeth-yos*
At what time is the rubbish collected?	¿A qué hora recogen la basura? *a keh ora rekohen la basoora?*

APARTMENTS

You may see:

Se alquila	**For rent**
Piso	**flat**
Apartamento	**apartment**
Chalet	**chalet**
Casa de campo	**country house**
Urbanización	**residential area**

- The cost of renting an apartment depends very much on location, size and how well equipped it is. Check out the details on the Internet or in a brochure before you decide.

- Apartments are usually rented out for a fortnight (**quincena**) or a month.

- Blocks of apartments usually have communal areas (gardens, swimming pools) which are subject to regulations for their use. Make sure you know them.

- The traditional siesta period during the early afternoon is generally observed amongst Spanish holidaymakers. Try to keep the noise down about this time if you are not sleeping.

- Many cookers are equipped with a combination of gas rings and electric rings. Many do not have a grill as we know it.

I would like an apartment...	Quiero un apartamento... *kee-yerro oon apartamento...*
...with one bedroom	...de un dormitorio *deh oon dormeetor-yo*
...for two people	...para dos personas *para dos pairsonas*
...for a month	...para un mes *para oon mes*
What floor is it on?	¿En qué piso está? *en keh peeso esta?*
I prefer the first floor/the top floor	Prefiero el primer piso/ el último piso *pref-yerro el preemair peeso/* *el oolteemo peeso*
How many beds are there?	¿Cuántas camas hay? *kwantas kamas I?*
How many bedrooms are there?	¿Cuántos dormitorios hay? *kwantos dormitor-yos I?*
Is...included?	¿Está incluido/a...? *esta eenklooeedo/a...?*
...everything	...todo *todo*
...the gas	...el gas *el gas*
...the water	...el agua *el agwa*

...electricity	...la electricidad *la elektreetheedad*
...the rubbish collection	...la recogida de basura *la rekoheeda deh basoora*
...the cleaning	...la limpieza *la limp-yetha*
Does it have...?	¿Tiene...? *tee-yenneh...?*
...a grill	...parrilla *paree-ya*
...a water heater	...calentador *kalentador*
...central heating	...calefacción *kalefakth-yon*
...air conditioning	...aire acondicionado *I-reh akondeeth-yonaddo*
Is it fully equipped?	¿Está equipado completo? *esta ekeepado kompletto?*
Is it electric/gas?	¿Es eléctrico/de gas? *es elektreeko/deh gas?*
Is/are there...?	¿Hay...? *I...?*
...bedclothes	...ropa de cama *ropa deh kama*
...crockery	...vajilla *bahee-ya*
...cutlery	...cubiertos *koob-yairtos*
...any furniture	...muebles *mweb-les*
...towels	...toallas *to-al-yas*

...a washing machine	...lavadora *labadora*
...dishwasher	...lavavajillas/lavaplatos *lababahee-yas/labaplattos*
...a (children's) swimming pool	...piscina (infantil) *pistheena (infanteel)*
I'm going...	Me voy... *meh boy...*
...now	...ahora *a-ora*
...this afternoon/this evening	...esta tarde *esta tardeh*
...tomorrow	...mañana *man-yana*
The bill, please	La cuenta, por favor *la kwenta, por fabbor*

PROBLEMS

There isn't any gas/(hot) water	No hay gas/agua (caliente) *no I gas/agwa (kal-yenteh)*
The...is not working	...no funciona *no foonth-yona*
The...is broken	...está roto/a *esta roto/a*
...air conditioning	El aire acondicionado... *el I-reh akondeeth-yonado...*
...cooker	La cocina... *la kotheena...*
...light	La luz... *la looth...*
...telephone	El teléfono... *el telefono...*

...basin	El lavabo... *el lababo...*
...sink	El fregadero... *el fregadero...*
...bath	El baño... *el banyo...*
...toilet	El wáter... *el batair...*
...shower	La ducha... *la doocha...*
Can you repair it?	¿Puede repararlo/la? *pwedeh repararlo/la?*
How much do I owe you?	¿Cuánto le debo? *kwanto leh debbo?*

You may hear:

No hay habitaciones *no I abeetathyon-es*	There aren't any rooms
No queda sitio *no keda seetyo*	There is no room
No hay plazas libres *no I plathas leebres*	There are no places
¿Para cuántas noches? *para kwantas noches?*	For how many nights?
¿Cuánto tiempo va a quedarse? *kwanto tee-yempo ba a kedarseh?*	How long are you staying?
¿Para cuántas personas? *para kwantas pairsonas?*	For how many people?
Está todo incluido *esta todo inklooeedo*	Everything is included
Firme aquí, por favor *feermeh akee por fabbor*	Sign here, please

¿Puede rellenar esta ficha?
pwedeh reh-yen-ar esta feecha?

Could you fill in this form?

¿Me deja su pasaporte,
por favor?
*meh deh-ha soo pasaporteh,
por fabbor?*

Could you give me your passport
please?

No puedo ir (hoy)
no pwedo eer (oy)

I can't go (today)

No puedo repararlo
no pwedo repararlo

I can't repair it

EATING OUT

If you are unable to find a meal in a restaurant because of the time, there are usually plenty of bars available for food.

- Eating and drinking in bars and restaurants is very much an integral part of Spanish everyday life. Children are welcome.

- Bars and cafeterias are open for most of the day until late at night. Restaurants generally serve meals between 1 o'clock and 3.30 for lunch and from about 9 o'clock until 11 o'clock for the evening meal. Times vary, and in most tourist areas restaurants open earlier and close later. If you are unable to find a meal in a restaurant because of the time, there are usually plenty of bars available for food.

- Generally the service in Spanish restaurants and bars is very efficient and the food of good quality. Prices must be displayed by law. Look for the *Menú del Día* sign for the most economical meal. Restaurants are categorised by a fork symbol, from one to five forks, and cafeterias by a cup symbol. Expect to pay corresponding prices in top restaurants and cafeterias.

- It is customary practice to include a small tip (between 5% and 10%) in most bars and restaurants even though most bills carry the sign *Servicio incluido* (service charge included). You will also see *IVA incluido* on your bill. This is the equivalent of VAT.

- In most Spanish bars it is customary to pay your bill as you leave. Prices vary depending on whether you stand at the bar or sit at a table. It is not customary to sit at a table already partially occupied by customers.

- In some large modern bars (in airports or department stores) you are given a form as you enter. The waiter will complete this for you and you pay the cashier as you leave.

- Spaniards usually eat the vegetable and meat courses separately. *Platos combinados* combine them in one course, as the British do.

- If you are not satisfied with service or food ask for the *Hoja de Reclamaciones* (the complaints book) which all bars and restaurants are obliged to carry.

- Most bars offer 'tapas' or bar snacks which are displayed at the bar.

- You will also find fast food restaurants (*comida rápida*), or takeaway establishments (*comida para llevar*). Some of these offer a delivery service (*servicio a domicilio*).

You may see:

bar	bar
restaurante	restaurant

It is customary practice to include a small tip (between 5% and 10%) in most bars and restaurants even though most bills carry the sign *Servicio Incluido* (service charge included).

cafetería	luxury café also serving alcohol
cervecería	beer cellar
hamburguesería/pizzería	burger bar/pizzeria
autoservicio	self-service
tapas	bar snacks
meriendas	afternoon snacks
desayunos	breakfasts
comidas	meals
buffet libre	self-service buffet
menú del día	menu of the day
platos combinados	combined dishes (meat and vegetables on one plate)

It is not customary to sit at a table already partially occupied by customers.

AT THE BAR

Waiter!	¡Camarero! *kamarerro!*
Waitress!	¡Camarera! *kamarerra!*
Excuse me, please	Oiga, por favor *oyga, por fabbor*
a cup/a mug of	una taza de *oona tatha deh*
a glass of	un vaso de *oon basso deh*
a bottle of	una botella de *oona botelya deh*
a jug of	una jarra de *oona harra deh*
half a bottle	media botella *medya botelya*

a can/a tin	una lata *oona latta*

NON-ALCOHOLIC DRINKS

I'd like...	Quiero... *kee-yerro...*
...a black coffee	...un café solo *oon kafeh solo*
...a white coffee	...un café con leche *oon kafeh kon lecheh*
...a decaffeinated coffee (with milk)	...un descafeinado (con leche) *oon deskafeynado (kon lecheh)*
...a tea (with milk/lemon)	...un té (con leche/limón) *oon teh (kon lecheh/leemon)*
with cold milk	con leche fría *kon lecheh freea*
with hot milk	con leche caliente *kon lecheh kal-yenteh*
...a glass of milk	...un vaso de leche *oon basso deh lecheh*
...a (strawberry) milk shake	...un batido (de fresa) *oon bateedo (deh frehsa)*
...a carbonated/natural mineral water	...un agua mineral con gas/ sin gas *oon agwa meeneral kon gas/ seen gas*
...a coca cola	...una coca cola *oona koka kola*
...a lemon drink	...una limonada *oona leemonada*
...an orange drink	...un naranjada *oona naranhada*

...a lemonade	...una gaseosa
	oona gas-yosa
...a tonic	...una tónica
	oona tonnika
a/an...juice	un zumo de...
	oon thoomo deh...
...apple	...manzana
	manthana
...grapefruit	...pomelo
	pomelo
...orange	...naranja
	naranha
...pineapple	...piña
	peenya
...tomato	...tomate
	tomateh

ALCOHOLIC DRINKS

Could you give me...	Póngame...
	pongameh...
...a beer	...una cerveza
	oona thairbetha
...a cider	...una sidra
	oona seedra
...a red wine	...un vino tinto
	oon beeno teento
...a white wine	...un vino blanco
	oon beeno blanko
...a rosé wine	...un vino rosado
	oon beeno rosado
...a house wine	...un vino de la casa
	oon beeno deh la kassa

...a sherry	...un jerez *oon hereth*
...(a glass of) champagne/ sparkling wine	...(una copa de) champán/cava *(oona kopa deh) champan/kaba*
...a brandy/cognac	...un coñac *oon konyak*
...a gin	...una ginebra *oona heenebra*
...a gin and tonic	...un gin tonic *oon jeentoneek*
...a vodka and orange	...un vodka con naranja *oon bodka kon naranha*
...a rum	...un ron *oon ron*
...a rum and coke	...un cubata *oon koobata*
...a liqueur	...un licor *oon leekor*
...a (Scotch) whisky	...un whisky (escocés) *oon weeskee (eskothes)*
with ice	con hielo *kon yelo*
with water	con agua *kon agwa*
with soda	con soda *kon soda*
neat/on its own	solo/a *solo/a*
sweet	dulce *dooltheh*
dry	seco *sekko*

TRY THESE SPECIAL DRINKS
Non-alcoholic

un café largo *oon kafeh largo*	a weak coffee with lots of water
un cortado *oon kortado*	a coffee with a drop of milk
un café con hielo *oon kafeh kon yelo*	coffee with ice
un chocolate (con churros) *oon chokolateh kon chooros)*	hot, thick chocolate (with fritters)
una horchata *oona orchata*	a drink made of nuts
un granizado (de limón/ de café) *oon graneethado deh leemon/deh kafeh*	drink served with crushed ice

Alcoholic

sangría *sangreea*	a drink made with wine, lemon and fruit
vino de Málaga *beeno deh malaga*	sweet wine
un moscatel *oon moskatel*	a sweet wine served with desserts and sweets or biscuits
una manzanilla *oona manthanee-ya*	dry sherry from the South of Spain (also means 'camomile tea')

SNACKS

A...sandwich/roll, please	un sandwich/bocadillo... por favor *oon sandwich/bokadee-yo... por fabbor*
...cheese	...de queso *deh kesso*

...ham	...de jamón *deh hamon*
...toasted	...tostado *tostado*
...salami	...de salchichón *deh salcheechon*
...spicy sausage	...de chorizo *deh choreetho*
a hamburger	una hamburguesa *oona amboorgessa*
a portion/two portions of...	una ración de/dos raciones de... *oona rath-yon deh/dos rath-yones deh...*
olives	aceitunas *athaytoonas*
squid	calamares *kalamares*

TRY THESE SPECIALITIES

ensaladilla rusa *ensaladeeya roosa*	Russian salad, made with potatoes, vegetables and mayonnaise sauce
gambas (al ajillo) *gambas (al aheeyo)*	prawns (in garlic sauce)
jamón serrano *hamon serranno*	cured ham

RESTAURANT

I'd like to reserve a table for...	Quiero reservar una mesa para... *kee-yerro resairbar oona messa para...*
...two	...dos *dos*
...eight o'clock	...las ocho *las ocho*

...tonight	...esta noche *esta nocheh*
...tomorrow	...mañana *man-yana*
I've reserved a table in the name of...	He reservado una mesa a nombre de... *eh resairbado oona messa a nombreh deh...*
I prefer that table	Prefiero aquella mesa *pref-yerro akel-ya messa*
Are there any free tables?	¿Hay mesas libres? *I messas leebres?*
There are five of us	Somos cinco *somos theenko*

You may hear:

No hay mesas libres *no I messas leebres*	There are no free tables
¿Para cuántas personas? *para kwantas pairsonas?*	For how many people?
Tendrán que esperar *tendran keh esperar*	You will have to wait
Pasen por aquí *passen por akee*	Could you come this way?

I'd like...	Quiero... *kee-yerro...*
...the menu of the day	...el menú del día *el menoo del deea*
...the tourist menu	...el menú turístico *el menoo tooreesteeko*
...the menu	...la carta *la karta*

...the buffet	...el buffet libre
	el boofeh leebreh
...a typical, local dish	...un plato típico de aquí
	oon platto teepeeko deh akee
...something vegetarian	...algo vegetariano
	algo beh-hetareeano
...the wine list	...la lista de vinos
	la leesta deh beenos
What do you recommend?	¿Qué me recomienda?
	keh meh rekom-yenda?
What is this?	¿Qué es esto?
	keh es esto?
Has this got fish/meat?	¿Tiene esto pescado/carne?
	tee-yenneh esto peskado/karneh?

You may hear:

Le recomiendo...	I recommend...
leh rekom-yendo...	
No nos queda	We haven't got any left
no nos keda	
En seguida se lo cambio	I'll change it immediately
en segeeda seh lo kamb-yo	

Could you bring...?	¿Puede traer...?
	pwedeh trlair...?
...some bread	...pan
	pan
...pepper	...pimienta
	pim-yenta
...salt	...sal
	sal
...sugar	...azúcar
	athookar

...water	...agua
	agwa
...a fork	...un tenedor
	oon tenedor
...a glass	...un vaso
	oon basso
...a knife	...un cuchillo
	oon koochee-yo
...a serviette	...una servilleta
	oona sairbee-yetta
...a spoon	...una cuchara
	oona koochara

You may hear:

¿Qué tomará/tomarán de
primero/de segundo (plato)?
*keh tomara/tomaran deh
preemero/deh segoondo (plato)?*

What will you have for the
first/second course?

¿Quiere algo de postre?
kee-yerreh algo deh postreh?

Would you like something
for dessert?

¿Para beber?
para bebair?

To drink?

¿Le/les gusta?
leh/les goosta?

Do you like it?

¿Está todo bien?
esta todo bee-yen?

Is everything OK?

ORDERING

For the first course I'd like...

De primer plato quiero...
deh preemair platto kee-yerro...

...mixed salad

...ensalada mixta
ensalada meexta

...plain omelette

...tortilla francesa
tortee-ya franthessa

...fish soup

...sopa de pescado
sopa deh peskado

• For others see page 50.

For the main course,...

De segundo plato...
deh segoondo plato...

...(lamb) chops

...chuletas (de cordero)
choolettas (deh kordero)

...roast chicken

...pollo asado
poyo asado

...steak and chips

...filete con patatas fritas
feeleteh kon patatas freetas

• For others see page 51.

For sweet...

De postre...
deh postreh...

...fresh fruit

...fruta del tiempo
froota del tee-yempo

...creme caramel

...flan
flan

...ice cream

...helado
elado

• For others see page 52.

You may see:

especialidad de la casa	house speciality
primer plato	starter (first dish)
segundo plato	main dish
postre	sweet/dessert
bebidas	drinks
plato del día	dish of the day
platos combinados	complete meals on a plate

menú a la carta	à la carte menu
menú del día	menu of the day
menú turístico	tourist menu
buffet libre	buffet
lista de vinos	wine list
entradas	starters
primeros platos	first courses
entremeses	starters/hors d'oeuvres
ensaladas	salads
sopa	soups
huevos	eggs
tortillas	omelettes
verduras	vegetables
pescados	fish
mariscos	sea food
carnes	meat
quesos	cheeses
pastelería	cakes/sweets
helados	ice cream
frutas	fruit
cubierto	cover charge
servicio incluido	service included

PRIMER PLATO

FIRST COURSE

arroz a la cubana
aroth a la koobana

rice with fried eggs, fried
bananas in tomato sauce

caldo
kaldo

meat and vegetable broth

cocido (madrileño)
kotheedo (madreelenyo)

a stew made of chick peas and meat

consomé (con yema/al jerez)
konsomeh (kon yema/al hereth)

chicken broth (with egg yolk/with sherry)

gazpacho
gathpacho

a cold vegetable soup made with tomatoes, cucumber, peppers, onion and garlic

huevos al plato
webbos al platto

fried eggs

menestra de verduras
menestra deh bairdooras

mixed fried vegetables with ham

paella de mariscos
pl-eya deh mareeskos

seafood paella

paella valenciana
pl-eya balenthee-yana

paella made with chicken, seafood and vegetables

pescaditos fritos
peskadeetos freetos

fried small fish

pulpo (a la gallega)
poolpo (a la ga-yega)

octopus (with sweet chilli and olive oil)

sopa de pescado
sopa deh peskado

fish soup

tortilla de patata
tortee-ya deh patata

Spanish omelette (made with potatoes and onion)

una empanadilla
oona empanadee-ya

a savoury-filled pastry

pimientos rellenos
peem-yentos reyenos

stuffed peppers

SEGUNDO PLATO

SECOND COURSE

albóndigas
albondeegas

meat balls

almejas a la marinera
almeh-has a la mareenera

clams in white wine sauce

callos a la madrileña
ka-yos a la madreelenya

tripe in piquant sauce

chuletas a la brasa
choolettas a la brassa

barbecued chops

cochinillo asado
kocheenee-yo asado

roast piglet

conejo (con alioli)
koneh-ho (kon aleeolee)

rabbit (with garlic mayonnaise)

merluza a la vasca
mairlootha a la baska

hake in béchamel and asparagus sauce

parrillada (de pescado y marisco)
paree-yada deh peskado ee mareesko

mixed grill (fish and seafood)

pollo al ajillo
poyo al ahee-yo

chicken fried with garlic

riñones al jerez
reen-yones al hereth

kidneys in sherry

trucha a la navarra/con jamón
troocha a la nabara/kon hamon

trout filled with ham

POSTRE

DESSERT

crema catalana
kremma katalana

thick custard with burnt sugar on top

macedonia de frutas
mathedonya deh frootas

fruit salad

melocotón con vino
melokoton kon beeno

peaches marinated in wine

natillas
natee-yas

custard

turrón
tooron

nougat (eaten mainly at Christmas)

WAYS OF COOKING FOOD

ahumado *aoomado*	smoked
al ajillo *al ahee-yo*	with garlic
a la plancha *a la plancha*	grilled
asado *asado*	roast
bien hecho *bee-yen echo*	well done
caliente *kal-yenteh*	hot
cocido *kotheedo*	boiled
con guarnición *kon gwarneeth-yon*	accompanied by vegetables and/or chips
crudo *kroodo*	raw
del tiempo *del tee-yempo*	of the season
duro *dooro*	hard boiled
en escabeche *en eskabecheh*	marinated/pickled
frío *freeo*	cold
frito *freeto*	fried
medio *med-yo*	medium
poco hecho *poko echo*	rare

relleno
reyeno

stuffed/filled

PROBLEMS

I didn't ask for that

Yo no he pedido eso
yo no eh pedeedo eso

This isn't for me

Esto no es para mí
esto no es para mee

Could you heat it up a bit more?

¿Puede calentarlo un poco más?
pwedeh kalentarlo oon poko mas?

It's a bit...

Está un poco...
esta oon poko...

...cold

...frío
freeo

...underdone

...crudo
kroodo

...burnt

...quemado
kemado

I don't think this is right

Creo que esto no está bien
kray-o keh esto no esta bee-yen

This bill isn't mine/is wrong

Esta cuenta no es la mía/
está equivocada
*esta kwenta no es la meea/
esta ekeebokada*

I didn't have that. Could
you change it?

No he tomado eso. ¿Puede
cambiarlo?
*no eh tomado eso. pwedeh
kambee-yarlo?*

You may hear:

Le traigo otro
leh trIgo otro

I'll bring you another

Se lo caliento
seh lo kal-yento

I'll heat it up

ENTERTAINMENT AND SPORT

- Cinema is very popular in Spain and as well as showing all the current Hollywood releases, you will find cinemas showing other films from all over the world and films from Spain's own thriving film industry. Cinemas often open at 4 or 5 pm and show films every two hours, depending on the length of the film. Check in the newspaper or on advertising hoardings (*cartelera* means film and theatre listings).

- In most towns, cinemas have reduced prices one day a week (*el día del espectador*), usually Monday or Wednesday.

- Most foreign films are dubbed into Spanish. Some are shown in their original version (*versión original VO*) and subtitled (*con subtítulos*). The authorities make recommendations as

In most towns, cinemas have reduced prices one day a week (*el día del espectador*), usually Monday or Wednesday.

to the suitability of films to different age groups.
Look for the following:
apta para todos los públicos (equivalent of a 'U' certificate),
mayores de 7/13/18 años ('7', '13', '18' certificate).

The bullfighting season runs from March to October and fights normally take place on Sundays.

- As well as getting you entrance to a club or disco, the ticket is normally valid for one drink. Subsequent drinks can be rather expensive.

- Beware of 'invitations' (*invitaciones*) to clubs and discos. These get you in but may not get you a drink so you may end up spending the same as for a normal entrance fee.

- The bullfighting season runs from March to October and fights normally take place on Sundays. Check the billboards or the local press as each bullring only holds a few fights during the season.

- In addition, every town and village in Spain has its annual *fiesta* and it is during this that some form of bullfighting or bull running (through the streets) takes place. The most famous of these is the July *feria* in Pamplona in northern Spain.

- There are also many cultural events in most towns in spring and summer, often in the open air, such as music concerts, dance, or theatre.

- Entrance to museums is not usually free, although international student card holders may pay reduced rates. Some museums have free entry on certain days or after a certain time in the afternoon. Check opening times in the local press. Some museums close on one day of the week.

cinema	el cine *el theeneh*
theatre	el teatro *el tay-atro*
nightclub	el club *el kloob*
nightclub/dance hall	la sala de fiestas *la salla deh fee-yestas*
disco	la discoteca *la deeskotekka*
One ticket, please	Una entrada, por favor *oona entrada, por fabbor*
One child's ticket	Una entrada de niño *oona entrada deh neenyo*
I'd like to reserve 4 tickets	Quiero reservar 4 entradas *kee-yerro resairbar kwatro entradas*
How much is it?	¿Cuánto es? *kwanto es?*
Do you have tickets for the 7 o'clock performance?	¿Hay entradas para las siete? *I entradas para las see-yetteh?*
Is there a discount...?	¿Hay descuento...? *I deskwento...?*
...today	...hoy *oy*
...for students	...para estudiantes *para estood-yantes*
...for pensioners	...para pensionistas *para pens-yoneestas*
...for children	...para los niños *para los neenyos*
When does...open?	¿Cuándo abre...? *kwando abreh...?*

When does...close?	¿Cuándo cierra...?
	kwando thee-yera...?
...the discotheque	...la discoteca
	la deeskoteka
...the sports centre	...el polideportivo
	el poleedeporteevo

AT THE CINEMA AND THEATRE

What time is...?	¿A qué hora es...?
	a keh ora es...?
...the (afternoon) showing	...la sesión (de tarde)
	la ses-yon (deh tardeh)
...the film	...la película
	la peleekoola
...the play	...la obra
	la obra
...the (evening) performance/show	...la función (de noche)
	la funth-yon (deh nocheh)
...the concert	...el concierto
	el konth-yairto
...the opera	...la ópera
	la opera
I'd like...	Quiero...
	kee-yerro
...stalls (orchestra)	...platea
	plateh-a
...circle (mezzanine)	...anfiteatro
	anfeetay-atro
...a (5) euro ticket	...una entrada de (cinco) euros
	oona entrada deh theenko euros
Are they numbered?	¿Son numeradas?
	son noomeradas?

at the front/back	delante/detrás
	delanteh/detras
in the middle	en el medio
	en el med-yo
I want a programme, please	Un programa, por favor
	oon programa, por fabbor

DISCOTHEQUES AND NIGHTCLUBS

Is there...?	¿Hay...?
	I...?
...a show	...espectáculo
	espektakoolo
...a music group	...algún grupo musical
	algoon groopo mooseekal
Is there a drink included?	¿Está incluida la consumición?
	esta inklooeeda la konsoomeeth-yon?
I have this invitation	Tengo esta invitación
	tengo esta inbeetath-yon
Do you have to wear evening dress?	¿Hay que ir con traje de noche/ de etiqueta?
	I keh eer kon traheh deh nocheh/ deh eteeketa?

OTHER USEFUL EXPRESSIONS

Where is the cloakroom?	¿Dónde está el guardarropa?
	dondeh esta el gwardaropa?
Where are the toilets?	¿Dónde están los servicios?
	dondeh estan los sairbeeth-yos?
I'd like to cancel a reservation	Quiero cancelar una reserva
	kee-yerro kanthelar oona resairba

AT A BULLFIGHT

Where is the bullring?	¿Dónde está la plaza de toros? *dondeh esta la platha deh toros?*
When is the bull fight?	¿Cuándo es la corrida? *kwando es la koreeda?*
A ticket...	Una entrada... *oona entrada...*
...in the shade	...de sombra *deh sombra*
...in the sun	...de sol *deh sol*
...in a good place	...en un buen sitio *en oon bwen seet-yo*
I'd like a cushion, please	Quiero una almohadilla, por favor *kee-yerro oona almoadee-ya, por fabbor*
How long does the bullfight last?	¿Cuánto tiempo dura la corrida? *kwanto tee-yempo doora la koreeda?*

You may hear:

No hay entradas *no I entradas*	We have no tickets left
Es gratis *es gratees*	It's free
No hacemos reservas *no athemos resairbas*	We don't take reservations
No tenemos venta anticipada *no tenemos benta anteetheepada*	We don't have advance sales

SPORTS

A ticket...	Una entrada... *oona entrada...*
...behind the goal	...de gol *deh gol*
...in the stand	...de tribuna *deh treeboona*
...on the terrace	...de general *deh heneral*
What time is the match?	¿A qué hora es el partido? *a keh ora es el parteedo?*
Can one...here?	¿Se puede...aquí? *seh pwedeh...akee?*
...dive	...bucear *bootheh-ar*
...fish	...pescar *peskar*
...go horse riding	...montar a caballo *montar a kaba-yo*
...go sailing	...navegar *nabegar*
...play tennis	...jugar al tenis *hoogar al tenees*
...ride a bicycle	...ir en bicicleta *eer en beetheekletta*
...swim	...nadar *naddar*
...windsurf	...hacer windsurf *athair weendsoorf*
...water-ski	...hacer esquí acuático *athair eskee akwateeko*
Is there...here/near here?	¿Hay...aquí/cerca? *I...akee/thairka?*

...a golf course	...un campo de golf
	oon kampo deh golf
...an (indoor) swimming pool	...una piscina (cubierta)
	oona pistheena (koob-yairta)
...a sports centre	...un polideportivo
	oon poleedeporteebo
...a tennis court	...una pista de tenis
	oona peesta deh tenees
Can I hire...?	¿Puedo alquilar...?
	pwedo alkeelar...?
...a bicycle	...una bicicleta
	oona beetheekletta
...a mountain bike	...una bicicleta de montaña
	oona beetheekletta deh montan-ya
...a (small) boat	...una barca
	oona barka
...a deck chair/a sun bed	...una hamaca
	oona amaka
...a pedal boat	...un patín
	oon pateen
...some skis	...unos esquís
	oonos eskees
...some ski boots	...unas botas de esquí
	oonas botas deh eskee
...a snowboard	...una tabla para la nieve
	oona tabla para la nee-yebeh
...a tennis racket	...una raqueta de tenis
	oona raketta deh tenees
...a windsurf board	...una tabla de windsurf
	oona tabla deh weendsoorf
...all the equipment	...todo el equipo
	todo el ekeepo

Do you have to pay to get in/become a member?

¿Hay que pagar para entrar/hacerse socio?
I keh pagar para entrar/athairseh soth-yo?

I would like...lessons

Quiero clases de...
kee-yerro klasses deh...

...tennis

...tenis
tenees

...ski

...esquí
eskee

How much is it per hour/per day?

¿Cuánto es por hora/por día?
kwanto es por ora/por deea?

Is there a lifeguard/a Red Cross post?

¿Hay socorrista/un puesto de Cruz Roja?
I sokoreesta/oon pwesto deh krooth roha?

VISITING THE TOWN

Where is/are...?

¿Dónde está/están...?
dondeh esta/estan...?

...the castle

...el castillo
el kastee-yo

...the cathedral

...la catedral
la katedral

...the (open air) market

...el mercado (al aire libre)
el mairkado (al ayreh leebreh)

...the museum

...el museo
el mooseyo

...the (main) square

...la plaza (Mayor)
la platha (mI-or)

...the ruins

...las ruinas
las rooeenas

...the shops

...las tiendas
las tee-yendas

When do they open/close?
¿Cuándo abren/cierran?
kwando abren/thee-yeran?

Is it open (on Sundays)?
¿Está abierto (los domingos)?
esta ab-yairto (los domeengos)?

Can I take photos?
¿Se puede hacer fotos?
seh pwedeh athair fotos?

Do you have postcards?
¿Tiene postales?
tee-yenneh postales?

Can you recommend an
excursion?
¿Puede recomendarme una
excursión?
*pwedeh rekomendarmeh
oona exkoors-yon?*

How long does it last?
¿Cuánto dura?
kwanto doora?

• For directions and other enquiries, see page 14.

You may hear:

Tiene que dejar...aquí
tee-yenneh keh de-har...akee

You have to leave...here

...su bolso
soo bolso

...your bag

...su abrigo
soo abreego

...your coat

...su paraguas
soo paragwas

...your umbrella

¿Puede abrir su bolso?
pwedeh abreer soo bolso?

Could you open your bag?

No está permitido hacer fotos
no esta pairmeeteedo athair fotos

It's not permitted/allowed
to take pictures

Hay que ser socio
I keh sair soth-yo

You have to be a member

MEETING PEOPLE

- When meeting people, or saying goodbye, it is usual to shake hands.

- Members of the family and close friends often kiss each other on each cheek on meeting and saying goodbye.

- Spaniards use 'Please' (*por favor*) and 'Thank you' (*gracias*) less than English speakers and tend to be more direct in their speech. This is not a sign of rudeness. The normal response to *gracias* is *de nada* ('Don't mention it').

- When meeting people you don't know or in a formal situation, use *usted* when addressing them. Use *tú* to people you know or people of your own age in an informal situation (see 'How are you?' below).

Good morning	Buenos días *bwennos deeas*
Good afternoon/evening	Buenas tardes *bwennas tardes*
Good night	Buenas noches *bwennas noches*
Hello!	¡Hola! *ola!*
How are you? (formal)	¿Cómo está usted? *komo esta oosted?*
How are you? (informal)	¿Qué tal (estás)? *keh tal (estas)?*
Very well, thanks	Muy bien, gracias *mwee bee-yen, grath-yas*
All right	Bien *bee-yen*
Not bad	Regular *regoolar*

When meeting people, or saying goodbye, it is usual to shake hands.

And you? (formal)	¿Y usted? *ee oosted?*
And you? (informal)	¿Y tú? *ee too?*
Is this seat occupied?	¿Está ocupada (esta silla)? *esta okoopada (esta see-ya)?*

You may hear:

Está... *esta...*	It's...
...libre *leebreh*	...free
...ocupado *okoopado*	...occupied

I am/my name is...	Me llamo... *meh yamo...*
What's your name? (formal)	¿Cómo se llama usted? *komo seh yama oosted?*
What's your name? (informal)	¿Cómo te llamas? *komo teh yamas?*
Pleased to meet you	Mucho gusto *moocho goosto*
One moment, please	Un momento, por favor *oon momento, por fabbor*
It doesn't matter	No importa *no eemporta*
I don't understand	No comprendo *no komprendo*
Could you...?	¿Puede...? *pwedeh...?*
...repeat that	...repetirlo *repeteerlo*

...speak more slowly
...hablar más despacio
ablar mas despath-yo

...translate it into English
...traducirlo al inglés
tradootheerlo al in-gles

I don't speak Spanish
No hablo español
no ablo espanyol

I speak a little Spanish
Hablo un poco de español
ablo oon poko deh espanyol

Do you speak English?
¿Habla inglés?
abla ingles?

What is this called in Spanish?
¿Cómo se llama esto en español?
komo seh yama esto en espanyol?

This is...
Éste/ésta es...
esteh/esta es...

...my husband
...mi marido
mee mareedo

...my fiancé/boyfriend
...mi novio
mee nobyo

...my friend (male)
...mi amigo
mee ameego

...my son
...mi hijo
mee ee-ho

...my wife
...mi esposa
mee esposa

...my fiancée/girlfriend
...mi novia
mee nobya

...my friend (female)
...mi amiga
mee ameega

...my daughter
...mi hija
mee ee-ha

I'm...
Soy...
soy...

...American	...americano/a *amereekano/a*
...Australian	...australiano/a *owstral-yano/a*
...Canadian	...canadiense *kanad-yenseh*
...English	...inglés/inglesa *in-gles/inglessa*
...Irish	...irlandés/irlandesa *eerlandes/eerlandessa*
...Scottish	...escocés/escocesa *eskothes/eskothessa*
...Welsh	...galés/galesa *gales/galessa*
Are you (Spanish)? (formal)	¿Es usted (español/española)? *es oosted (espanyol/espanyola)?*
Are you (South American)? (informal)	¿Eres (sudamericano/a)? *e-res (soodamereekano/a)?*
Where do you come from? (informal)	¿De dónde eres? *deh dondeh e-res?*
I live...	Vivo... *beebo...*
...in London	...en Londres *en londres*
...in New York	...en Nueva York *en nweba york*
...in the north of England	...en el norte de Inglaterra *en el norteh deh inglaterra*
I have...	Tengo... *tengo...*
...a son/a daughter	...un hijo/una hija *oon ee-ho/oona ee-ha*

...two children	...dos hijos *dos ee-hos*
I don't have any children	No tengo hijos *no tengo ee-hos*
I'm on holiday	Estoy de vacaciones *estoy deh bakath-yones*
I work here	Trabajo aquí *traba-ho akee*
I'm a student	Soy estudiante *soy estood-yanteh*
And you? (formal)	¿Y usted? *ee oosted?*
And you? (informal)	¿Y tú? *ee too?*
Would you like to...? (informal)	¿Quieres...? *kee-yerres...?*
...dance	...bailar *bIlar*
...have something to drink/eat	...tomar algo *tomar algo*
...come out with me (tomorrow)	...salir conmigo (mañana) *saleer konmeego (man-yana)*
...go out for dinner/supper	...ir a comer/cenar *eer a komair/thennar*
I'll treat you (informal)	Te invito *teh eenbeeto*
Where shall we meet?	¿Dónde quedamos? *dondeh kedamos?*
Can I call you/pick you up? (informal)	¿Puedo llamarte/ir a buscarte? *pwedo yamarteh/eer a booskarteh?*
No thanks	No gracias *no grath-yas*

I can't	No puedo *no pwedo*
Goodbye	Adiós *ad-yos*
See you later	Hasta luego *asta lwego*
See you soon	Hasta pronto *asta pronto*

BUSINESS EXPRESSIONS

I'm...	Soy... *soy...*
...Mr (Smith)	...el señor (Smith) *el senyor (smeeth)*
...Mrs (Smith)	...la señora (Smith) *la senyora (smeeth)*
...Miss (Smith)	...la señorita (Smith) *la senyoreeta (smeeth)*
I'm from the...Company	Soy de la Compañía... *soy deh la kompan-yeea...*
I have an appointment with...	Tengo una cita con... *tengo oona theeta kon...*
Could I...?	¿Podría...? *podreea...?*
...see Mr (Pérez)	...ver al señor (Pérez) *bair al senyor (pereth)*
...speak to Miss (Pérez)	...hablar con la señorita (Pérez) *ablar kon la senyoreeta (pereth)*
Here is my card	Aquí tiene mi tarjeta *akee tee-yenneh mee tarhetta*
I'm sorry I'm late	Siento llegar tarde *see-yento yegar tardeh*
I'm in the hotel (Goya)	Estoy en el hotel (Goya) *estoy en el otel (goya)*

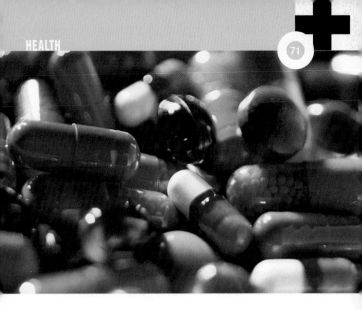

HEALTH

- In Spain you can obtain free medical attention provided you take with you an E111 form, which you can get from the post office in the UK before you depart.

- Dentists are very expensive and only provide limited services within the National Health Service.

- In case of accident or emergency go to an emergency first aid centre (*Casa de Socorro*) or the nearest hospital (*hospital*) and look for the *Urgencias*.

In Spain you can obtain free medical attention provided you take with you an E111 form, which you can get from the post office in the UK before you depart.

- If you require treatment on the road, there are first aid posts (*puesto de socorro de Cruz Roja*) at regular intervals.

- If you need a doctor look for:

  médico (doctor)

  consultorio (doctor's surgery)

  ambulatorio (health centre)

- If you need an ambulance look for: *ambulancia*.

- A *practicante* is a qualified nurse permitted to give injections.

- Medicines can be obtained from a chemist (*farmacia*). You have to pay a percentage of the prescription unless you are a pensioner. Outside each chemist there is a list of local chemists which are open 24 hours a day (*farmacia de guardia*).

- Chemists are identified by a red or green cross symbol.

- At night and sometimes even during the day, you may have to ring a doorbell to gain entry.

ASKING FOR HELP

Can you help me, please?	Ayúdeme, por favor *ayoodehmeh, por fabbor*
I don't speak Spanish	No hablo español *no ablo espanyol*
Do you speak English?	¿Habla inglés? *abla ingles?*
I need...	Necesito... *netheseeto...*
...a doctor	...un médico *oon mediko*

...an interpreter	...un intérprete *oon eentairpreteh*
...to go to hospital	...ir al hospital *eer al ospeetal*
Where is...?	¿Dónde está...? *dondeh esta...?*
...the hospital	...el hospital *el ospeetal*
...the doctor's surgery	...la consulta (del doctor) *la konsoolta (del doktor)*
...the 'emergencies' entrance	...la entrada de urgencias *la entrada deh oorhenth-yas*
It's urgent/serious	Es urgente/grave *es oorhenteh/grabeh*
I am ill/injured	Estoy enfermo/a/herido/a *estoy enfairmo/a/ereedo/a*
I've had an accident	He tenido un accidente *eh teneedo oon aktheedenteh*
Can you call an ambulance/ take me to hospital?	¿Puede llamar a una ambulancia/ llevarme al hospital? *pwedeh yamar a oona amboolanth- ya/yebbarmeh al ospeetal?*
Is there a doctor?	¿Hay un médico...? *I oon mediko...?*
...here	...aquí *akee*
...in the hotel	...en el hotel *en el otel*
...in the campsite	...en el camping *en el kampeeng*
Is there a nurse/a first-aid box?	¿Hay enfermera/botiquín? *I enfairmera/boteekeen?*

Can the doctor come...?	¿Puede venir el doctor...? *pwedeh beneer el doktor...?*
...now	...ahora *a-ora*
...today	...hoy *oy*
...as soon as possible	...cuanto antes *kwanto antes*
My address is...	Mi dirección es... *mee deerekth-yon es...*

AT THE DOCTOR'S

What time is the surgery open?	¿A qué hora es la visita? *a keh ora es la biseeta?*
Could you give me an appointment with...?	¿Me da hora para...? *meh da ora para...?*
...the doctor (GP)	...el médico (de cabecera) *el mediko (deh kabetherra)*
...eye specialist	...el oculista *el okooleesta*
...the gynaecologist	...el ginecólogo *el heenehkologo*
...the dentist	...el dentista *el denteesta*
...the specialist	...el especialista *el espeth-yaleesta*
It hurts me here	Me duele aquí *meh dwelleh akee*
My...hurts	Me duele... *meh dwelleh...*
...ankle	...el tobillo *el tobee-yo*

...arm	...el brazo *el bratho*
...back	...la espalda *la espalda*
...breast/chest	...el pecho *el pecho*
...ear	...el oído *el oeedo*
...eye	...el ojo *el oho*
...finger	...el dedo *el dedo*
...foot	...el pie *el pee-yeh*
...hand	...la mano *la mano*
...head	...la cabeza *la kabetha*
...knee	...la rodilla *la rodee-ya*
...leg	...la pierna *la pee-yairna*
...lung	...el pulmón *el poolmon*
...mouth	...la boca *la boka*
...neck	...el cuello *el kweyo*
...penis	...el pene *el peneh*
...shoulder	...el hombro *el ombro*

...stomach	...el estómago *el estomago*
...throat	...la garganta *la garganta*
...vagina	...la vagina *la baheena*
...wrist	...la muñeca *la moon-yekka*
My...hurt	Me duelen... *meh dwellen...*
...joints	...las articulaciones *las arteekoolath-yones*
It hurts	Me duele... *meh dwelleh...*
...a lot	...mucho *moocho*
...a little	...un poco *oon poko*
...all the time	...continuamente *konteenwamenteh*
...sometimes	...a veces *a beth-es*
It's been hurting...	Me duele... *meh dwelleh...*
...since yesterday	...desde ayer *desdeh ayair*
...for two days	...desde hace dos días *desdeh atheh dos deeas*
...for a few hours	...desde hace unas horas *desdeh atheh oonas oras*
It's a sharp pain	Es un dolor agudo *es oon dolor agoodo*

| I feel... | Estoy...
| | *estoy...* |

...ill
...enfermo/a
enfairmo/a

...bad
...mal
mal

...faint
...mareado/a
mareyado/a

...weak
...débil
debeel

...worse
...peor
peyor

I am constipated
Estoy estreñido/a
estoy estren-yeedo/a

I have a cold
Estoy resfriado/a
estoy resfreeado/a

I have...
Tengo...
tengo...

...cramps
...calambres
kalambres

...diarrhoea
...diarrea
deearea

...insomnia
...insomnio
eensomnyo

...a migraine
...jaqueca
hakekka

...a rash
...un sarpullido
oon sarpoo-yeedo

...a stiff neck
...tortícolis
torteekolees

I think I have...
Creo que tengo...
kray-o keh tengo...

...broken something	...una fractura *oona fraktoora*
...the flu	...la gripe *la greepeh*
...food poisoning	...una intoxicación *oona eentoxeekath-yon*
...indigestion	...una indigestión *oona eendee-hest-yon*
...an infection	...una infección *oona eenfekth-yon*
...sinusitis	...sinusitis *seenooseetees*
...sun stroke	...una insolación *oona eensolath-yon*
...a temperature	...fiebre *fee-yebbreh*
...an allergy	...una alergia *oona alairhee-a*
It itches	Me pica *meh peeka*
I can't breathe properly/ move (my arm)/walk	No puedo respirar bien/ mover (el brazo)/andar *no pwedo respeerar bee-yen/ mobair (el bratho)/andar*
It's infected/swollen	Está infectado/a/inflamado/a *esta eenfektado/a/eenflamado/a*

WHAT'S HAPPENED?

I've fallen over	Me he caído *meh eh ka-yeedo*
I've burned myself	Me he quemado *meh eh kemado*

I've cut myself	Me he cortado
	meh eh kortado
I've bumped myself	Me he dado un golpe
	meh eh dado oon golpeh
I've taken this	He tomado esto
	eh tomado esto
I've twisted my ankle	me he torcido el tobillo
	meh eh tortheedo el tobee-yo
My friend...	Mi amigo/a...
	mee ameego/a
...is injured	...está herido/a
	esta ereedo/a
...is ill	...está enfermo/a
	esta enfairmo
...is unconscious	...está inconsciente
	esta eenkonsth-yenteh
...has fainted	...se ha desmayado
	seh a desmayado
...has had a (heart) attack	...ha tenido un ataque (al corazón)
	a teneedo oon atakeh (al korathon)
I've been stung/bitten by...	Me ha picado/mordido...
	meh a peekado/mordeedo...
...something	...algo
	algo
...an insect	...un insecto
	oon eensekto
...a mosquito	...un mosquito
	oon moskeeto
...a wasp	...una avispa
	oona abeespa
...a bee	...una abeja
	oona abeh-ha

...a dog	...un perro
	oon perro
...a snake	...una serpiente
	oona sairp-yenteh

GENERAL CONDITIONS

I have...	Tengo...
	tengo...
...asthma	...asma
	asma
...diabetes	...diabetes
	deeabetes
...high/low blood pressure	...la tensión alta/baja
	la tens-yon alta/baha
I'm allergic to penicillin/ antibiotics	Tengo alergia a la penicilina/ los antibióticos
	tengo alairheea a la peneetheeleena/ los anteebeeoteekos
I take this/this medicine	Tomo esto/esta medicina
	tomo esto/esta medeetheena
I'm (3 months) pregnant	Estoy embarazada (de tres meses)
	estoy embarathada (deh tres meses)
I have a heart condition	Estoy enfermo/a del corazón
	estoy enfairmo/a del korathon
I had a heart attack	Tuve un infarto
	toobeh oon eenfarto

QUESTIONS

Could you give me something...?	¿Puede darme algo...?
	pwedeh darmeh algo...?
...for the pain	...para el dolor
	para el dolor

...to sleep	...para dormir *para dormeer*
I (don't) want...	(No) quiero... *(no) kee-yerro...*
...injections	...inyecciones *eenyekth-yones*
...suppositories	...supositorios *sooposeetor-yos*
When do I have to take it?	¿Cuándo tengo que tomarlo? *kwando tengo keh tomarlo?*
Do I have to stay in bed?	¿Tengo que guardar cama? *tengo keh gwardar kama?*
When can I...?	¿Cuándo puedo...? *kwando pwedo...?*
...sunbathe	...tomar el sol *tomar el sol*
...bathe	...bañarme *banyarmeh*

AT THE OPTICIAN'S

Can you repair my glasses?	¿Puede arreglar mis gafas? *pwedeh areglar mees gafas?*
I would like glasses/ contact lenses	Quiero unas gafas/ lentes de contacto *kee-yerro oonas gaffas/ lentes deh kontakto*
I've something in this eye	Tengo algo en este ojo *tengo algo en esteh oho*

AT THE DENTIST'S

It aches here

Me duele aquí
meh dwelleh akee

This tooth/this molar/my gum aches

Este diente/esta muela/
la encía me duele
*esteh dee-yenteh/esta mwella/
la entheea meh dwelleh*

A filling has fallen out

Se me ha caído un empaste
se meh a ka-yeedo oon empasteh

I have an abscess

Tengo un flemón
tengo oon flemon

Please don't take out my tooth

No me saque la muela, por favor
no meh sakeh la mwella, por fabbor

Can you fix my dentures?

¿Puede arreglar la dentadura?
pwedeh areglar la dentadoora?

PAYING

How much do I owe you?

¿Cuánto le debo?
kwanto leh debbo?

Do I have to pay something now?

¿Tengo que pagar algo ahora?
tengo keh pagar algo a-ora?

I have this insurance

Tengo este seguro
tengo esteh segooro

Could you...?

¿Puede...?
pwedeh...?

...give me a receipt

...darme un recibo
darmeh oon retheebo

...give me a medical certificate

...darme un certificado médico
darmeh oon thairteefeekado mediko

...fill this in

...rellenar esto
reyenar esto

You may hear:

¿Dónde le duele?
dondeh le dwelleh?

Where does it hurt?

Tome esto
tomeh esto

Take this

cada (cuatro) horas
kada (kwatro) oras

every (four) hours

antes/después de las comidas
antes/despwes deh las komeedas

before/after meals

(tres) veces al día
(tres) bethes al deea

(three) times a day

Guarde cama
gwardeh kama

Stay in bed

No se bañe
no seh banyeh

Don't bathe

Tiene que ir al hospital
tee-yeneh keh eer al ospeetal

You have to go to the hospital

Vuelva mañana
bwelba man-yana

Come back tomorrow

TRAVEL

BY TRAIN

- The Spanish national rail network is known as RENFE (*Red Nacional de Ferrocarriles Españoles*). It is state-operated and claims to be the most inexpensive, most modern and highest performing rail system in Europe. The service offered by RENFE is divided into four main sectors: local or urban services (*Cercanías*); regional services (*Regional*) offering services within or across regions up to 400 kilometres in distance; main line services (*Grandes Líneas*) for distances above 400 kilometres; and the high speed train services (*AVE – Líneas de Alta Velocidad*) offering high speed luxury services between Madrid and the south of Spain and imminently to the north and east. There are a number of different train designs used on the *Grandes Líneas* and *AVE* routes, often depending on where you are travelling. The *AVE*, *Alaris*, *Lanzaderas* and *Talgo 200* appear on the *AVE* routes, and the *Talgo*, *Euromed*, *Tren Estrella*, *Diurnos*, *Intercity*, *Trenhotel* (overnight), *ARCO* and *Altaria* are some of the names you will see on the *Grandes Líneas* routes.

- When buying a ticket for a long journey it is advisable to make a seat reservation at least 24 hours before your journey. If you are too late to reserve a seat, ask the ticket collector (*revisor/revisora*) to help you find an unreserved seat.

- You can purchase tickets for long-distance routes up to 60 days before travelling.

- Look out for discount offers. Some of the more common ones are: Children up to 3 years of age pay nothing. Children between the ages of 4 and 13 get a 40% discount. If you are between the age of 12 and 26 you are entitled to a young person's railcard (*Carnet joven*) which gets you a 20% discount. If you buy a return ticket (*ida y vuelta*) and make the return journey within 60 days, you get 20% discount. Groups of more than 10 persons purchasing tickets together may get between 10% and 30% discount depending on the journey, and there are also discounts for small groups occupying a complete cabin in one of the overnight trains (*trenhotel*). Discounts are also available under the *Bonocity* scheme for 4 long-distance journeys. If you intend to do a lot of rail travel, check out the Inter Rail card before you depart.

- Main stations are equipped with automatic ticket vending machines (*autoventa de billetes*) which issue tickets for all journeys and accept credit cards.

 When buying a ticket for a long journey it is advisable to make a seat reservation at least 24 hours before your journey.

- Spanish law requires that passengers under the age of 16 may only travel alone if they carry written authorisation from a parent or guardian.

- Further information can be obtained from the Spanish National Tourist Office (22–23 Manchester Square, London W1M 5AP), and from RENFE on the Internet (www.renfe.es).

Do you have...?	¿Tienen...?
	tee-yennen...?
...a railway timetable	...un horario de trenes
	oon orareeo deh tren-es
...information about discounts	...información de descuentos
	eenformath-yon deh deskwentos

Children up to 3 years of age pay nothing.

You may see:

Estación	Station
Largo recorrido	Long distance
Grandes líneas	Long distance lines
Interurbano	Inter-City
Cercanías	Local trains
Llegadas	Arrivals
Salidas	Departures
Procedencia...	Train from...
Destino	Destination
Andén/vía	Platform
Consigna	Left luggage
Despacho de billetes/taquilla	Ticket office
Venta inmediata	Tickets on sale for immediate use
Venta anticipada	Advance ticket sales

Entrada	**Entrance**
Salida	**Exit**
Facturación de equipajes	**Luggage check-in**
Horarios	**Timetable**
Sala de espera	**Waiting room**

What trains are there for (Madrid)...?
¿Qué trenes hay a (Madrid)...?
keh tren-es I a (madreed)...?

...today
...hoy
oy

...tomorrow
...mañana
man-yana

...on Sunday
...el domingo
el domeengo

• For times, see page 147.

What time does...leave?
¿A qué hora sale...?
a keh ora saleh...?

...the next train
...el próximo tren
el proxeemo tren

...the first train
...el primer tren
el preemair tren

...the last train
...el último tren
el ooltimmo tren

Does it stop in all the stations?
¿Para en todas las estaciones?
para en todas las estath-yones?

How long does it take?
¿Cuánto tiempo tarda?
kwanto tee-yempo tarda?

Spanish law requires that passengers under the age of 16 may only travel alone if they carry written authorisation from a parent or guardian.

Do I have to change trains/ make a connection?	¿Hay que cambiar de tren/ hacer transbordo? *I keh kamb-yar deh tren/ athair transbordo?*
Is there a supplement?	¿Hay suplemento? *I soopleemento?*
Is/are there...?	¿Hay...? *I...?*
...a bar	...bar *bar*
...couchettes	...literas *leeterras*
...a restaurant car	...restaurante *restowranteh*
...sleeping compartments	...coche-cama *kocheh-kama*
At what time does the bar close/open?	¿A qué hora cierra/abre el bar? *a keh ora thee-yerra/abreh el bar?*
Is there a discount for...?	¿Hay descuento para...? *I deskwento para...?*
...children	...niños *neenyos*
...students	...estudiantes *estood-yantes*
...retired people	...jubilados *hoobeelados*
Where is...?	¿Dónde está...? *dondeh esta...?*
...the left luggage office	...la consigna *la konseegna*
...the luggage check-in	...la facturación de equipajes *la faktoorath-yon deh ekeepa-hes*

...platform (4)	...el andén (4) *el anden (kwatro)*
...the ticket window	...la taquilla *la takee-ya*
...the waiting room	...la sala de espera *la sala deh esperra*
Are there any luggage trolleys?	¿Hay carritos para el equipaje? *I kareetos para el ekeepaheh?*

• For directions and asking the way, see page 14.

Which platform does it leave from?	¿De qué andén sale? *deh keh anden saleh?*
Is it delayed?	¿Lleva retraso? *yebba retrasso?*

BUYING TICKETS

Two tickets...	Dos billetes... *dos beeyet-es...*
...to Barcelona	...para Barcelona *para barthelona*
...for the three o'clock Talgo	...para el Talgo de las tres *para el talgo deh las tres*
Can I reserve a seat?	¿Se puede hacer reserva? *seh pwedeh athair resairba?*
A...ticket, please	Un billete..., por favor *oon beeyeteh..., por fabbor*
single	de ida *deh eeda*
return	de ida y vuelta *deh eeda ee bwelta*
first/second class	primera/segunda clase *preemerra/segoonda klasseh*
smoker	fumador *foomador*

non-smoker	no fumador *no foomador*
in couchette	en litera *en leeterra*
in a sleeping compartment	en coche-cama *en kocheh-kama*
and one child's	y uno de niño *ee oono deh neenyo*
How much is that?	¿Cuánto es? *kwanto es?*
Could you write it?	¿Puede escribirlo? *pwedeh eskreebeerlo?*
I have a credit/discount card	Tengo tarjeta de crédito/descuento *tengo tarhetta deh kreditto/deskwento*

LUGGAGE

I would like...	Quiero... *kee-yerro...*
...to check this in	...facturar esto *faktoorar esto*
...to leave this	...dejar esto *deh-har esto*
Could you help me with my luggage?	¿Puede ayudarme con el equipaje? *pwedeh ayoodarmeh kon el ekeepaheh?*

ON THE PLATFORM

Is the (Madrid) train running late?	¿Tiene retraso el tren (para Madrid)? *tee-yeneh retrasso el tren (para Madreed)?*

When will it arrive?	¿Cuándo llegará? *kwando yegara?*
Is this...?	¿Es éste...? *es esteh...?*
...the train for (Malaga)	...el tren para (Málaga) *el tren para (malaga)*
...the platform for (Barcelona)	...el andén para (Barcelona) *el anden para (barthelona)*
...the second class carriage	...el coche de segunda *el kocheh de segoonda*
Where is the...carriage?	¿Dónde está el coche...? *dondeh esta el kocheh...?*
...first class	...de primera *deh preemerra*
...restaurant	...restaurante *restowranteh*
I don't have a reservation	No tengo reserva *no tengo resairba*
Excuse me/I'm sorry...	Perdone... *Pairdoneh...*
Is this seat taken?	¿Está ocupado (este asiento)? *esta okoopado (esteh as-yento)?*
Could you...?	¿Puede...? *pwedeh...?*
...find me a seat	...buscarme un asiento *booskarmeh oon as-yento*
...tell me when we get to (Malaga)	...avisarme cuando lleguemos a (Málaga) *abeesarmeh kwando yegemmos a (malaga)*
Have we arrived?	¿Ya hemos llegado? *ya ehmos yegado?*

This is my seat	Éste es mi asiento *esteh es mee as-yento*
This seat is taken	Este asiento está ocupado *esteh as-yento esta okoopado*

You may hear:

Tiene que cambiar *tee-yenneh keh kamb-yar*	You have to change
Compruebe los datos *komprwebbeh los dattos*	Check the details (on your ticket)
Hay suplemento *I sooplehmento*	There is a supplementary charge
Lleva (media hora) de retraso *yebba (med-ya ora) deh retrasso*	It's (half an hour) late

BY COACH

- Most of the signs and information boards found in bus and coach stations are the same as for railway stations (see **By Train** section on page 86).

- Coach travel is cheaper than train travel and the main routes provide a comfortable, fast service. It is advisable to book in advance.

- All towns and villages are linked by a bus or coach service.

Where is the bus station?	¿Dónde está la estación de autobuses? *dondeh esta la estath-yon deh owtobooses?*
When are there buses to (Madrid)?	¿Cuándo hay autobuses a (Madrid)? *kwando I owtobooses a (madreed)?*

A ticket for (Madrid)	Un billete para (Madrid)
	oon beeyeteh para (madreed)
What time does it leave/arrive?	¿A qué hora sale/llega?
	a keh ora saleh/yegga?
Are you going by motorway?	¿Va por autopista?
	ba por owtopeesta?
Does it have...?	¿Tiene...?
	tee-yenneh...?
...air conditioning	...aire acondicionado
	I-reh akondeeth-yonado
...a toilet	...servicio
	sairbeeth-yo
Are there any spare places?	¿Hay plazas libres?
	I plathas leebres?
Where does it stop?	¿Dónde para?
	dondeh para?

• For other expressions, see **By Train**, page 87.

BY BUS AND UNDERGROUND

• Spanish towns have a frequent, reliable and relatively cheap bus service (*autobús*). Buses are operated on a flat-fare, 'Pay-as-you-enter' basis and passengers either pay the driver, or insert a single ticket or a multi-journey ticket into an automatic machine.

• Single tickets can be purchased from the driver or from a vendor found at the main bus stops or termini. Most passengers buy a multifare-ticket (*bonobús*) which can be purchased from ticket vendors, banks, Savings Banks (*Caja de Ahorros*) and some big department stores. They may not be purchased from bus drivers. In Madrid, these tickets may also be used on the buses and the metro system.

In the Canary Islands a bus is known as *guagua* (pronounced wa-wa). Multi-tickets are known as *bono guagua*.

- Bus routes are indicated by number (eg *línea 40*) and the route is displayed at each bus stop (*parada*). Buses display the route number and names of the departure and terminus points.

- In the Canary Islands a bus is known as *guagua* (pronounced *wa-wa*). Multi-tickets are known as *bono guagua*.

- Underground systems exist in Madrid, Barcelona and Bilbao. Look for the *METRO* sign. The various lines are indicated by colours and numbers (eg *línea 2*) and direction is indicated by the last station on the line (*dirección*).

- Underground stations open at 6 am and close at 1.30 am.

- Tickets must be inserted into machines at the beginning of the journey. Keep your ticket with you throughout your journey.

- In Madrid, a special travel card (*bono transporte*) can be purchased. This is valid for all three transport systems (Bus, Metro and Rail) and is available from tobacconists (*estanco*), and tube and train station ticket points. A monthly ticket (*cupón*) should be purchased with this card and the two are used in conjunction for any journey within the capital within a zone system. You will need your passport to apply for your monthly *tarjeta*.

Could you give me...?	Deme... *demeh...*
...a book of tickets	...un bonobús/ un metrobús *on bonoboos/oon metroboos*
...a (bus) pass	...un abono *oon abono*

In Madrid, a special travel card (*bono transporte*) can be purchased. This is valid for all three transport systems (Bus, Metro and Rail) and is available from tobacconists (*estanco*), and tube and train station ticket points.

...a travel card	...una tarjeta (multiviaje) *oona tarhetta (moolteebee-yaheh)*
...a monthly ticket	...un cupón mensual *oon koopon menswal*
Is this the stop for the number 4 bus?	¿Es ésta la parada del autobús número 4? *es esta la parada del owtoboos noomero kwatro?*
Does this bus go (to the centre)?	¿Va este autobús (al centro)? *ba esteh owtoboos (al thentro)?*

• For numbers see page 144.

Do you have a plan (map)...?	¿Tiene un plano...? *tee-yenneh oon plano...?*
...of the underground	...del metro *del metro*
...of bus routes	...de autobuses *deh owtobooses*
Which line is it to (Atocha Station)?	¿Qué línea es a (la estación Atocha)? *keh leen-ya es a (la estath-yon atocha)?*
Do I have to change?	¿Tengo que cambiar? *tengo keh kamb-yar?*
Where?	¿Dónde? *dondeh?*
Do you have a timetable?	¿Tiene un horario? *tee-yenneh oon orareeo?*

BY CAR

• For car hire see page 18.

• Spanish law requires you to carry your driving licence at all times. If you have a European style UK licence (pink or pink/green) you do not require an International Driving Permit. If you have one of the old-style green licences, you will need an International Driving Permit.

- Your British insurance will give you only third party cover in Spain, whatever cover is valid in the UK. Your insurance company may recommend issue of a green card to extend this cover. You should carry this at all times, and it is also advisable to carry your vehicle registration document.

- If you drive any vehicle over 75cc capacity you must be at least 18 years of age. For motorcycles of less than 75cc no permit is necessary and the minimum age is 16.

- A GB sticker should be clearly displayed on your vehicle.

- Seat belts are obligatory at all times. Children up to the age of 3 must be seated in a proper child seat. Children under the age of 12 are not allowed to sit in the front passenger seat.

- Crash helmets must be worn by all motorcyclists, and dipped headlights used at all times.

- It is against the law to carry a spare can of petrol.

- It is compulsory to carry a spare set of light bulbs for each light of the car.

- All Spanish motorways operate on a toll system (*peaje*). Prices vary from motorway to motorway. Look for the signs *manual* or *automático* depending on whether you have the right change.

 Spanish law requires you to carry your driving licence at all times. If you have a European style UK licence (pink or pink/green) you do not require an International Driving Permit. If you have one of the old-style green licences, you will need an International Driving Permit.

- Motorways are indicated by 'A' (for *autopista*) followed by the number.

- Main roads are indicated by 'N' (*nacional*) followed by the number (sometimes given in Roman numerals), and secondary roads are indicated by the letter 'C' (*comarcal*) followed by the number.

- The maximum speed limit is 120 kph on motorways (*autopista*), 100 kph on main roads (*carretera nacional*) and 90 kph on other roads. Limits vary between 40 kph and 60 kph in towns. Many towns now have traffic lights at the point where the speed limit comes into force, which automatically turn to red if your car is approaching at above the town speed limit, obliging you to stop. The minimum permitted speed on motorways is 60 kph (kph = kilometres per hour).

- The permitted alcohol limit in Spain is lower than in the UK. You may be asked to take a breathalyser test.

- Hitch-hiking is legal but difficult and inadvisable.

- The *Guardia Civil de Tráfico* patrol the open road. These are different police from the *Guardia Municipal*, who are in charge of traffic in towns. Police have the authority to fine motorists on the spot and to impound your car if you are unable to pay.

- In case of an accident there are a number of Red Cross posts (*puestos de Cruz Roja*) attended round the clock.

- Where possible, avoid holiday weekends. It is quite normal for drivers to sound their horn behind you when traffic lights change to green. Flashing one's headlights usually means 'Look out!' rather than 'After you'. Spanish drivers do not give way to the same extent as drivers in the UK. It is customary for drivers of large vehicles to flash their nearside

A GB sticker should be clearly displayed on your vehicle.

indicator when they consider it is safe for the car behind to overtake.

AT THE PETROL STATION

• Most service stations (*gasolineras*) operate a self-service system, although there are still many which are attended. Some stations are completely automated with cash machines available for customers to key in the amount they wish to spend before filling up. Petrol is sold unleaded (*sin plomo*), or leaded (*super* for the equivalent of 4 star; *normal* for the equivalent of 2 star). Diesel (*gas oil* or *gasóleo*) is available. Prices will not normally vary as they are regulated by the government. They are generally similar to those in the UK. Some petrol stations will not give change, especially at night, for security reasons.

Where is there...?	¿Dónde hay...? *dondeh I...?*
...a car park	...un parking *oon parkeeng*
...a garage	...un garage *oon garaheh*
...a petrol station (gas station)	...una gasolinera/ estación de servicio *oona gasoleenerra/ estathyon deh serbeethyo*
Fill her up!	Lleno, por favor *yenno, por fabbor*
(Ten) litres of...	(Diez) litros de... *(dee-yeth) leetros deh...*
Twenty euros of...	Veinte euros de... *beyn-teh euros deh...*

...unleaded petrol	...gasolina sin plomo *gasoleena seen plomo*
...4 star	...super *soopair*
...2/3 star	...normal *normal*
...diesel	...gasoil *gasoil*
A litre of oil, please	Deme un litro de aceite *dehme oon leetro deh atheyteh*
How much is it?	¿Cuánto es? *kwanto es?*
Could you check...?	¿Puede mirar...? *pwedeh meerar...?*
...the battery	...la batería *la batereea*
...the oil	...el aceite *el atheyteh*
...the radiator	...el radiador *el rad-yador*
...the tyres	...los neumáticos *los noomateekos*
...the windscreen wipers	...los limpiaparabrisas *los leemp-ya-parabreesas*
Could you...?	¿Puede...? *pwedeh...?*
...clean the windows	...limpiar los cristales *leemp-yar los kreestales*
...wash the car	...lavar el coche *labar el kocheh*

The permitted alcohol limit in Spain is lower than in the UK. You may be asked to take a breathalyser test.

PROBLEMS

Flashing one's headlights usually means 'Look out!' rather than 'After you'.

I don't have a spare wheel	No tengo rueda de repuesto *no tengo rooedda deh repwesto*
I don't have spare light bulbs	No tengo luces de repuesto *no tengo loothes deh repwesto*
I've run out of petrol	Me he quedado sin gasolina *meh eh kedado seen gasoleena*
Have you got a petrol can?	¿Tiene una lata? *tee-yenneh oona lata?*
My car won't start	Mi coche no arranca *mee kocheh no arranka*
I've had...	He tenido... *eh teneedo...*
...an accident	...un accidente *oon aktheedenteh*
...a breakdown	...una avería *oona abereea*
...a puncture	...un pinchazo *oon peenchatho*
There's a funny noise	Hay un ruido extraño *I oon rooeedo extranyo*
Could you change the wheel/the bulb?	¿Puede cambiar la rueda/la bombilla? *pwedeh kamb-yar la rooeda/la bombee-ya?*
The engine has overheated	Se ha calentado el motor *seh a kalentado el motor*
How long will it take?	¿Cuánto tardará? *kwanto tardara?*

It's urgent	Es urgente *es oorhenteh*
I'm...	Estoy... *estoy...*
...(10) kilometres away	...a (10) kilómetros *a (dee-yeth) keelometros*
...on the motorway	...en la autopista *en la owtopeesta*
...on the (Madrid) road	...en la carretera de (Madrid) *en la kareterra deh (madreed)*
...at kilometre 20	...en el kilómetro 20 *en el keelometro beynteh*
It's a Renault car	Es un Renault *es oon renaw*
The registration number is...	la matrícula es... *la matreekoola es...*
• For numbers, see page 144.	
Can you...?	¿Puede...? *pwedeh...?*
...help me	...ayudarme *ayoodarmeh*
...take me to (a petrol station)	...llevarme a (una gasolinera) *yebbarmeh a (oona gasoleenera)*
...send a mechanic	...mandar a un mecánico *mandar a oon mekaneeko*
...send a breakdown lorry	...mandar una grúa *mandar oona grooa*
...call an ambulance	...llamar una ambulancia *yammar oona amboolanth-ya*

Some petrol stations will not give change, especially at night, for security reasons.

AT THE GARAGE

• Look for the signs *garaje* and *taller*.

Do you do repairs?	¿Hacen reparaciones? *athen reparath-yones?*
I don't know what is wrong with it	No sé qué le pasa *no seh keh leh pasa*
I'd like a service	Quiero una puesta a punto *kee-yerro oona pwesta a poonto*
The...is broken/doesn't work	...está roto/no funciona *esta roto/no foonth-yona*
...windscreen	El parabrisas... *el parabreesas...*
...seatbelt	El cinturón... *el theentooron...*
...horn	El claxon... *el klaxon...*
...heater	El calentador... *el kalentador*
Can you check...?	¿Puede mirar...? *pwedeh meerar...?*
...the accelerator	...el acelerador *el athelerador*
...the brakes	...los frenos *los frennos*
...the carburettor	...el carburador *el karboorador*
...the clutch	...el embrague *el embrageh*
...the engine	...el motor *el motor*
...the exhaust pipe	...el tubo de escape *el toobo deh eskapeh*

...the fan belt	...la correa del ventilador *la korrea del benteelad*
...the gear box	...la caja de cambios *la kaha deh kamb-yos*
...the handbrake	...el freno de mano *el frenno deh mano*
...the indicators	...los intermitentes *los eentairmeetentes*
...the petrol pump	...la bomba de gasolina *la bomba deh gasoleena*
...the spark plugs	...las bujías *las booheeas*
...the starter (motor)	...el motor de arranque *el motor deh arrankeh*
...the steering	...la dirección *la deerekth-yon*
...the suspension	...la suspensión *la soospens-yon*
When will (the car) be ready?	¿Cuándo estará listo (el coche)? *kwando estara leesto (el koche)?*
This is the key...	Ésta es la llave... *esta es la yabbeh...*
...to the boot (trunk)	...de la maleta *deh la maletta*
...to the petrol tank	...del depósito de gasolina *del deposeeto deh gasoleena*
Could you give me an estimate/the bill	¿Puede darme un presupuesto/la factura? *pwedeh darmeh oon presoopwesto/la faktoora?*
Is VAT included?	¿Está incluido el IVA? *esta inklooeedo el eeba?*

Here are the documents	Aquí tiene mis documentos *akee tee-yenneh mees dokoomentos*
Can I have your documents, please?	¿Sus documentos, por favor? *soos dokoomentos, por fabbor?*

You may hear:

¿Dónde está? *dondeh esta?*	Where are you?
¿Qué marca de coche es? *keh marka deh kocheh es?*	What make of car is it?
¿Qué le pasa? *keh leh passa?*	What's wrong with it?
Tiene que dejarlo... *tee-yenneh keh deh-harlo...*	You must leave it...
...dos días *dos deeas*	...for two days
...hasta mañana *asta man-yana*	...until tomorrow

You may see:

badén permanente	in constant use (no parking)
calle cortada por obras	road closed for roadworks
carretera particular	private road
ceda el paso	give way
desvío	diversion
estacionamiento (limitado)	(restricted) parking
obras	roadworks
paso a nivel	level crossing
peatones	pedestrians
peaje	toll
prohibido aparcar	no parking

uso obligatorio cinturón de seguridad	seat belt compulsory
zona azul	no parking (blue zone)
zona peatonal	pedestrians only
encienda las luces/los faros	switch on lights
apague las luces/los faros	switch off lights
vehículos lentos	slow vehicles

SHOPPING

- Opening hours for most shops are from 9.30 or 10 am to 1 or 1.30 pm and again from 4 or 5 pm to 7.30 or 8.30 pm. Large department stores often adopt the same hours but do not close for lunch. Look for the sign *abierto* (open) or *cerrado* (closed).

- All large stores and most shops accept credit cards but there are still some smaller shops which may not have credit card facilities, as well as many smaller food shops.

- Gift wrapping of goods is customary in most Spanish shops where requested.

- In towns and cities it is the practice for some smaller shops (as well as bars and restaurants) to close for the month of July or August.

You will see the sign *cerrado por vacaciones* (closed for holidays). Alternatively, some shops close for the afternoon during the summer.

- The label PVP (*Precio de Venta al Público*) indicates retail price and *IVA incluido* indicates that the Spanish equivalent of VAT is included.

- Open air markets (*rastro* or *mercadillo*) are held once or twice a week in most Spanish towns and resorts.

- For currency see **Bank** section, page 125.

- Sales (*Rebajas, Liquidación*) take place in January/February and July/August.

- Some shops offer free delivery service (including food). This service will be indicated by the sign *Servicio a Domicilio*. You can also order from supermarkets and grocers by telephone.

HYPERMARKETS AND SUPERMARKETS

- Hypermarkets are usually found outside big towns and cities and sell everything from food and clothes to domestic appliances and car accessories. They are usually cheaper than supermarkets.

- On the way out be prepared for the security officer to ask to see inside any handbags you may have with you.

- Department stores:
  In larger towns and cities you will find department stores (*grandes almacenes*), the most famous of which is *El Corte Inglés*. These are the equivalent of the large department stores in the UK.

On the way out be prepared for the security officer to ask to see inside any handbags you may have with you.

I'm just looking, thanks	Estoy mirando, gracias
	estoy meerando, grath-yas
I'm next	Me toca a mí
	meh toka a mee
I'd like this	Quiero eso
	kee-yerro eso
Do you have...?	¿Tiene...?
	tee-yenneh...?
more	más
	mas
less	menos
	mennos

You may hear:

¿A quién le toca?	Who's next?
a kee-yen leh toka?	
El/la siguiente, por favor	Next, please
el/la seeg-yenteh, por fabbor	
¿Qué desea?	What would you like?
keh deseya?	
¿En qué puedo servirle?	How can I help you?
en keh pwedo sairbeerleh?	
¿Le atienden?	Are you being attended to?
leh at-yenden?	
No tenemos/no hay	We don't have any
no tenemmos/no I	
No me queda	I have none left
no meh kedda	
¿Cuánto quiere?	How much would you like?
kwanto kee-yerreh?	
¿Algo más?	Anything else?
algo mas?	
¿Se lo envuelvo?	Shall I wrap it?
seh lo enbwelbo?	

¿Quiere una bolsa?
kee-yerreh oona bolsa?

Would you like a bag?

Son quince euros
son keentheh euros

That will be 15 euros

¿Paga en efectivo o con tarjeta?
paga en efekteebo o kon tarhetta?

Are you paying by cash or by credit card?

Pague en caja
pageh en kaha

Please pay at the till

¿A dónde se lo enviamos?
a dondeh seh lo enbee-yamos?

Where shall we send it?

It's very expensive

Es muy caro
es mwee karro

I'd like something...

Quiero algo...
kee-yerro algo...

...bigger

...más grande
mas grandeh

...smaller

...más pequeño
mas peken-yo

...cheaper

...más barato
mas baratto

Nothing else

Nada más
nada mas

How much is it?

¿Cuánto es?
kwanto es?

Could you write it down?

¿Puede escribirlo?
pwedeh eskreebeerlo?

Do you accept credit cards?

¿Aceptan tarjetas de crédito?
atheptan tarhettas deh kredeeto?

Could you (gift) wrap it?

¿Puede envolverlo (para regalo)?
pwedeh enbolbairlo (para regalo)?

Do you have a bag?

¿Tiene una bolsa?
tee-yenneh oona bolsa?

| Could you send it to...? | ¿Puede enviarlo/la a...? |
| | *pwedeh enbee-yarlo/la a...?* |

You may see:

Autoservicio	Self-service
Entrada	Entrance
Salida	Way out/exit
Oferta	Special offer
Caja especial	Special till/checkout
(máximo cinco artículos)	(maximum of 5 items)
Caja	Checkout/till

SHOPPING FOR FOOD

- It is very common to do all your shopping in a covered market where you will find a range of stalls to meet your needs.

- Weights and measures: most food is bought by the kilo or fractions of a kilo or otherwise by grams.

- Liquids are bought by the litre. There are about two pints in a litre.

- See word list for individual items.

Can I have...	Deme...
	demeh...
I'd like...	Quiero...
	kee-yerro...
a kilo of...	un kilo de...
	oon keelo deh...
half a kilo of...	medio kilo de...
	med-yo keelo deh...

a packet of...	un paquete de... *oon paketteh deh...*
a jar of...	un bote/un tarro de... *oon boteh/oon tarro deh...*
a bottle of...	una botella de... *oona boteya deh...*
a box of...	una caja de... *oona kaha deh...*
a tin of...	una lata de... *oona lata deh...*
a dozen...	una docena de... *oona dothenna deh...*
half a dozen...	media docena de... *med-ya dothenna deh...*
a slice of...	una loncha de... *oona loncha deh...*
	una rodaja de... *oona rodaha deh...*

FRUIT AND VEGETABLES

• Look for the signs *Frutería/Verdulería* (greengrocers).

Brussels sprouts	coles de Bruselas *col-es deh broosellas*
leeks	puerros *pwerros*
(green/red) pepper	pimiento (verde/rojo) *pim-yento (bairdeh/roho)*
a head of garlic	una cabeza de ajos *oona kabetha deh ahos*
grapes (green/black)	uvas (blancas/negras) *oobas (blankas/neggras)*

AT THE GROCER'S

- Look for the signs *Comestibles* or *Alimentación*. These are shops which sell everything from tinned food to wine and bread.

decaffeinated/instant coffee	café descafeinado/instantáneo *kafeh deskafeynado/eenstantanyo*
(olive) oil	aceite (de oliva) *atheyteh (deh oleeba)*
(drinking) yogurt	yogur (para beber) *yogoor (para bebair)*
stock cubes	cubitos de caldo *koobeetos deh kaldo*
(powdered) milk	leche (en polvo) *lecheh (en polvo)*
tomato puree	tomate frito *tomateh freeto*
some tea bags	unas bolsitas de té *oonas bolseetas deh teh*
a bar of chocolate	una tableta de chocolate *oona tabletta deh chokolateh*

SNACKS AND APERITIFS

- Many of these snacks can be obtained in bars, as well as in shops. They are known generally as *tapas* and are sometimes included in the price of the drinks.

tuna fish (in oil)	atún (en aceite) *atoon (en atheyteh)*
green/black/stuffed olives	olivas verdes/negras/rellenas *oleebas bairdes/negras/reyennas*

Many of these snacks can be obtained in bars, as well as in shops. They are known generally as *tapas* and are sometimes included in the price of the drinks.

olives without the stone	olivas sin hueso
	oleebas seen wesso
cheese sticks	palitos de queso
	paleetos deh kesso
hazelnuts	avellanas
	abeyanas
peanuts	cacahuetes
	kakawettes
sunflower seeds	pipas
	peepas

AT THE BUTCHER'S AND DELICATESSEN

- Look for *Charcutería, Salchichería* (butcher's delicatessen). Also *embutidos* (cold meats, especially pork).

- You can buy this sort of thing in a grocer's store or in a *Mantequería* (delicatessen).

bacon	bacón/tocino
	bakon/totheeno
ham	jamón de york
	hammon deh york
pâté	paté
	pateh
cheese in portions	quesitos
	keseetos
...cheese	queso...
	kesso...
soft...	...blando
	blando
hard...	...duro
	dooro
mild...	...suave
	swabeh

strong...	...fuerte
	fwairteh
goat's	...de cabra
	deh kabra
round shaped, mild...	...de bola
	deh bola
hard (from ewe's milk)...	...manchego
	mancheggo

Spanish specialities

jamón serrano	cured/smoked ham
hamon serranno	
chorizo	spicy sausage
choreetho	
longaniza	spicy sausage with herbs
longaneetha	
butifarra	large sausage
booteefara	
morcilla	black pudding
morthee-ya	
mortadela	cold meat
mortadella	
requesón	cottage/curd cheese
rekehson	

AT THE BAKER'S

- Look for the signs *Panadería* (bakery), *Pan* (bread) and *Horno* (oven).

- Many bakers also sell milk and soft drinks, ice cream, cakes and sweets.

| a long loaf | una barra |
| | *oona barra* |

Many bakers also sell milk and soft drinks, ice cream, cakes and sweets.

a...loaf	un pan... *oon pan...*
...large	...grande *grandeh*
...medium	...mediano/a *med-yano/a*
...small	...pequeño/a *peken-yo/a*
sliced bread	pan de molde *pan deh moldeh*
a bread roll	un panecillo *oon panethee-yo*
a bun	un bollo *oon boyo*

MILK

• Look for *Lechería*. Milk is also sold in bakers, grocers or supermarkets but is not delivered to your door.

A bottle of...milk, please	Una botella de leche...por favor *oona botteya deh lecheh...por fabbor*
...full cream	...entera *enterra*
...semi-skimmed	...semidesnatada *semeedesnatada*
...skimmed	...desnatada *desnatada*

CAKES AND SWEETS

• Look for *Pastelería* (cake shop), *Confitería*, *Bombonería* or *Dulces*. They all sell sweets.

• A *Churrería* is a shop selling *churros* (fritters), *buñuelos* and crisps to take away.

- *Buñuelos* are another kind of fritter, round in shape.

- Cakes (*pasteles*) can be bought singly but it is more common to buy them by the half dozen (*media docena*), the dozen (*docena*) or by weight. A larger cake such as a birthday cake or a flan-type cake is known as *tarta*. A popular type of cake is the *tarta helada*, a cake made with ice cream. Types of cake often vary from region to region and there are also seasonal differences as well as cakes made for special festivals.

- If you don't know the name, point and say *Quiero eso, por favor*. If you want a cake typical of the region say *Quiero un pastel típico de aquí*.

Two euros worth of churros, please	dos euros de churros, por favor *dos euros deh chooros, por fabbor*
small candied egg yolks	yemas *yemmas*
chocolates	bombones *bombones*
mints	caramelos de menta *karamellos deh menta*

ICE CREAM

- In summer look for *Heladería* (Ice cream parlour) or *helados* (ice cream). You can also normally buy *horchata* (a drink made with tiger nuts) and *granizado* (a drink made with crushed ice and lemon or coffee) in these places.

a cornet	un barquillo *oon barkeeyo*

A *churro* is a long strip of fried dough sprinkled with sugar. They are best eaten when they are hot and are very popular dipped in hot chocolate (*chocolate con churros*).

a (chocolate) iced lolly	un polo (de bombón)
	oon polo (deh bombon)
a wafer	un corte
	oon korteh

MEAT

• Look for *Carnicería* (Butcher's).

loin	lomo
	lomo
steak	filete
	feeletteh
meat for stew	carne para estofado
	karneh para estofado
a joint for roasting	una pieza para asar
	oona pee-yetha para asar
I want it boneless/without fat	Lo quiero sin hueso/sin grasa
	lo kee-yerro seen wesso/seen grasa
minced meat	carne picada
	karneh peekada

CHICKEN AND POULTRY

whole	entero
	enterro
in pieces	a trozos
	a trothos
chicken breasts	pechugas de pollo
	pechoogas deh poyo
chicken legs	muslos de pollo
	mooslos deh poyo
chicken wings	alas de pollo
	alas deh poyo

FISH AND SEAFOOD

- Look for *Pescadería* (Fishmonger's), *Pescados* (fish) and *Mariscos* (seafood).

- Spain is very rich in fish and seafood. You will find many varieties that you may not have seen before and will want to try. Just point and say '*Ese pescado, por favor*' (That fish, please).

eels	anguilas *angeelas*
hake	merluza *mairlootha*
red mullet	salmonetes *salmonettes*
sprats	sardineta *sardeenetta*
whitebait	boquerones *bokehron-es*
(big) prawns	langostinos *langosteenos*
cod	bacalao *bakala-o*
sardines	sardinas *sardeenas*
squid	calamares *kalamar-es*
salmon	salmón *sal-mon*
sole	lenguado *len-gwado*

Spain is very rich in fish and seafood. You will find many varieties that you may not have seen before and will want to try.

prawns	gambas *gambas*
mussels	mejillones *mehee-yon-es*
clams	almejas *almehas*
Please, can you...?	Por favor, ¿puede...? *por fabbor, pwedeh...?*
...clean it	...limpiarlo *limp-yarlo*
...fillet it	...cortarlo a filetes *kortarlo a feelet-es*
...take the bones out	...quitar la raspa *keetar la raspa*

AT THE TOBACCONIST'S

• Look for *Estanco* or *Tabacos*, where you can buy tobacco, stamps, postcards and sweets. You can buy dark or light tobacco. The Spanish brand names are much cheaper than the imported brands.

A packet of cigarettes	Un paquete de cigarrillos *oon paketeh deh theegareeyos*
a box of matches	una caja de cerillas *oona kaha deh thereeyas*
a packet of cigars	un paquete de puros *oon paketeh deh pooros*
a stamp	un sello *oon selyo*
an envelope	un sobre *oon sobreh*
this postcard	esta postal *esta postal*
letter-writing paper	papel de carta *papel deh karta*

AT THE CHEMIST'S

- Look for *Farmacia* and a red or green cross symbol. There is a rota system of chemists which remain open for 24 hours (*Farmacia de Guardia*).

- Chemists sell medical supplies and a limited selection of toiletries. You will find a wide range of the latter in a *Perfumería* or *Droguería* (drugstore).

- See also page 74, **At the doctor's**.

I have this prescription	Tengo esta receta
	tengo esta rethetta
baby food	comida para niños
	komeeda para neenyos
insect repellent	loción para insectos
	loth-yon para insektos
plasters	tiritas
	teereetas
throat pastilles	pastillas para la garganta
	pasteeyas para la garganta
I'd like something for...	Quiero algo para...
	kee-yerro algo para...

BUYING TOILETRIES

- Look for *Perfumería* or *Droguería* (drugstore), sometimes called *Droguería-Perfumería*. These sell toiletries and also household goods.

handcream	crema para las manos
	kremma para las manos
lipsalve	cacao para los labios
	kakow para los lab-yos
make-up remover	crema limpiadora
	kremma leemp-yadora

| paper tissues | pañuelos de papel |
| | *panwellos deh papel* |

SELF-CATERING AND CAMPING EQUIPMENT

- Look for *Droguería* (see above), *Ferretería* (the nearest British
  equivalent is the hardware store) and *Deportes* (sports shop).
  Adaptors and other electrical goods can be bought in *Electro-
  domésticos* (electrical goods).

a tea cloth	un paño de cocina
	oon panyo deh kotheena
washing powder	detergente
	detair-henteh
washing-up liquid	lavavajillas
	lababahee-yas
an insecticide	un insecticida
	oon eensekteetheeda
kitchen roll	un rollo de papel de cocina
	oon royo deh papel deh kotheena
rubbish bags	bolsas de basura
	bolsas deh basoora
a scouring pad	un estropajo
	oon estropaho
tent pegs	estacas de camping
	estakas deh kampeeng

BEACH AND PHOTOGRAPHIC ITEMS

- You can buy beach items at sports shops, and general stores. Look
  for the sign *Artículos de Playa*.

- Photographic films are not bought in chemists. Look for
  photographic specialists and in the *Fotografía* section of
  department stores.

a black and white film	un rollo en blanco y negro *oon royo en blanko ee negro*
a colour film	un rollo en color *oon royo en kolor*
for prints	para fotos *para fotos*
for slides	para diapositivas *para deeaposeeteebas*
Please can you...?	Por favor, ¿puede...? *por fabbor pwedeh...?*
...develop the film	...revelar el rollo *rebelar el royo*
...load the camera	...poner el rollo *ponair el royo*
...take the film out	...sacar el rollo *sakkar el royo*
...repair the camera	...reparar la cámara *reparar la kamara*
The film is stuck	El rollo está atascado *el royo esta ataskado*
When will they be ready?	¿Cuándo estarán hechas? *kwando estaran echas?*

Photographic films are not bought in chemists. Look for photographic specialists and in the Fotografía section of department stores.

AT THE STATIONER'S

- If you wish to buy stationery, magazines, newspapers etc look for
  Librería (bookshop/stationers), *Papelería* (stationers), *Kiosco* (kiosk),
  or *Estanco* (tobacconist).

Where are the English
newspapers?

¿Dónde están los periódicos ingleses?
dondeh estan los peree-odikos ingleses?

Do you have books in
English?

¿Tienen libros en inglés?
tee-yenneh leebros en ingless?

Are there are English
magazines?

¿Hay revistas inglesas?
I rebeestas inglessas?

PRESENTS

- Look for *Regalos* (gifts), *Bazar* (bazaar), *Joyería* (jeweller's), *Tienda de
  Regalos* (gift shop), *Souvenirs*.

CLOTHES

- Look for *Moda, Confecciones Señora* (women's clothes shop),
  Confecciones Caballero (men's clothes shop), *Modas* (fashion
  clothes). For leather goods look for *Artículos de Piel* or *Cuero*.

- For sizes, colours, materials, patterns etc. see **Essential Information**.

I'd like size 40

Quiero la talla 40
kee-yerro la ta-ya kwarenta

Can I try it (them) on?

¿Puedo probármelo(s)?
pwedo probarmelo(s)?

Where is the fitting room?

¿Dónde está el probador?
dondeh esta el probador?

It doesn't (they don't) fit

No me va(n) bien
no me ba(n) bee-yen

I'll take it (them)

Me lo(s) quedo
meh lo(s) kedo

SHOES AND SHOE REPAIRS

• Look for *Zapatería, Calzados* (shoe shop) and *Zapatos* (shoes).

• For repairs look for *Reparaciones de Calzado* or *Zapatero*.

Do you have these shoes in black?	¿Tiene estos zapatos en negro? *tee-yenneh esos thapatos en neggro?*
Can you repair these shoes?	¿Puede reparar estos zapatos? *pwedeh reparar estos thapatos?*
Can you put on a new heel/sole?	¿Puede poner un tacón nuevo/una suela nueva? *pwedeh ponair oon takon nwebbo/oona swella nwebba?*
When will they be ready?	¿Cuándo estarán listos? *kwando estaran leestos?*
Do you have shoe polish?	¿Tiene betún? *tee-yenneh betoon?*

SERVICES

AT THE BANK

- Normal banking hours are from 9am to 2pm on weekdays and on Saturdays from 9am to 1pm, although some banks close on Saturdays during the summer. You can change money in normal banks (*Banco*) and also in a savings bank (*Caja de Ahorros*). For reasons of security many banks employ the use of an entry bell which customers press before they are let in. ATMs or cash machines (*cajeros automáticos*) are often found inside the bank and are accessed outside opening hours by using your credit or debit card which opens an automatic door to let you in to the cash machine section.

- When changing traveller's cheques or Eurocheques you will need to have your passport with you, though not if you want to change cash. Look for the sign *Cambio* or *Extranjero*. Banks display the exchange rates of most currencies. Look for the sign *Libra Esterlina* for pounds sterling and *Dólares* for dollars.

- The clerk will work out the exchange and commission (this varies from bank to bank) and will then send you to a till or window (*Caja* or *Ventanilla*) to collect your money. You can use credit or debit cards with your PIN to get money directly from cash machines. Check that the symbols (Visa, Cirrus, etc) on your cards appear on the cash machine.

- In some of the bigger cities there are branches of the major British banks. Check services available with your own bank before you travel.

Normal banking hours are from 9am to 2pm on weekdays and on Saturdays from 9am to 1pm, although some banks close on Saturdays during the summer.

- Currency: Spain is one of the member states of the European Community using the Euro. Coins (*monedas*) are in units of 1 and 2 euros. Units below 1 euro are called cents (*céntimos*), of which there are 100 in 1 euro. Coins are as follows: 50 (*céntimos*), 20, 10, 5, 2, 1. The front of the coins displays the same European standard motif, whilst the back has a motif of the country producing the coin. Any euro coin, no matter what its origin, can be used in any country which has the euro as its currency. Bank notes (*billetes*) come in denominations of 500, 200, 100, 50, 20, 10 and 5 euros. Unlike coins, they do not have country-specific designs or motifs. Everyone is obliged to display prices in euros. Note that the most common way of telling you how much something costs if it includes euros and cents, is to use the word *con* (with); for example: *Son dos euros con cincuenta* (that's two euros fifty cents), although you will also hear *dos euros cincuenta*.

Any euro coin, no matter what its origin, can be used in any country which has the euro as its currency.

I'd like to change…	Quiero cambiar…
	kee-yerro kamb-yar…
…these pounds (sterling)	…estas libras
	estas leebras
…these dollars	…estos dólares
	estos dolares
…this into euros	…esto en euros
	esto en euros
…this into pounds	…esto en libras
	esto en leebras
…this into dollars	…esto en dólares
	esto en dolares
I'd like to cash…	Quiero cobrar…
	kee-yerro kobrar…
…these traveller's cheques	…estos cheques de viaje
	estos chek-es deh bee-aheh

...these Eurocheques
...estos eurocheques
estos eurochek-es

...this cheque
...este cheque
esteh chekeh

What is the exchange rate?
¿A cómo está el cambio?
a komo esta el kamb-yo?

It's...
Son...
son...

...three hundred pounds
...trescientas libras
tres-thee-yentas leebras

...five hundred dollars
...quinientos dólares
keen-yentos dolares

• For numbers see page 144.

How much commission do you charge?
¿Cuánto cobran de comisión?
kwanto kobran deh komees-yon?

Do you want...?
¿Quiere...?
kee-yerreh...?

...my passport
...mi pasaporte
mee pasaporteh

...my Eurocheque card
...mi tarjeta Eurocheque
mee tarhetta eurochek-eh

Where do I sign?
¿Dónde firmo?
dondeh feermo?

Can you give me...
Deme...
dehmeh...

...small notes
...billetes pequeños
beeyet-es pekenyos

...coins
...moneda
monedda

...change
...cambio
kamb-yo

Can I use this card?	¿Puedo usar esta tarjeta? *pwedo oosar esta tarhetta?*
Could you call/fax my bank?	¿Puede llamar/mandar un fax a mi banco? *pwedeh yamar/mandar oon fax a mee banko?*
Has some money arrived for me?	¿Ha llegado una transferencia para mí? *a yegado oona transferenth-ya para mee?*
I've lost...	He perdido... *eh pairdeedo...*
...some traveller's cheques	...unos cheques de viaje *oonos chek-es deh bee-aheh*
...some Eurocheques	...unos Eurocheques *oonos eurochek-es*
...my (credit) card	...mi tarjeta (de crédito) *mee tarhetta (deh kreditto)*
...my cheque book	...mi talonario *mee talonar-yo*
I'd like to...	Quiero... *kee-yerro...*
...open a savings account	...abrir una cuenta de ahorro *abreer oona kwenta deh a-orro*
...open a current account	...abrir una cuenta corriente *abreer oona kwenta koree-yenteh*
...pay this into my account	...ingresar esto a mi cuenta *ingressar esto a mee kwenta*
...withdraw (1,000) euros from my account	...sacar (mil) euros de mi cuenta *sakar (meel) euros deh mee kwenta*

...transfer some money

...hacer una transferencia
athair oona transferenth-ya

...send a giro

...mandar un giro
mandar oon heero

Here is/are...

Aquí tiene...
akee tee-yenneh...

...the details

...los datos
los dattos

...my residence permit

...mi permiso de residencia
mee pairmeeso deh reseedenth-ya

Could you tell me the balance of my account?

¿Puede decirme el saldo de mi cuenta?
pwedeh detheermeh el saldo deh mee kwenta?

You may hear:

Firme aquí
feermeh akee

Sign here

Me da su carnet de identidad
meh da soo karneh deh identidad

Could you give me your ID card please?

Su pasaporte, por favor
soo pasaporteh, por fabbor

Your passport, please

Pase por caja/a la ventanilla de pagos
paseh por kaha/a la bentaneeya de pagos

Could you go to the till?

Este papel es para usted
esteh papel es para oosted

This paper is for you

¿Puede...?
pwedeh...?

Could you...?

...esperar un momento
esperar oon momento

...wait a moment

...rellenar esto
reyennar esto

...fill this out

¿Cómo se llama usted?
komo seh yama oosted?

What is your name?

BUSINESS EXPRESSIONS

I'd like to speak to...

Quisiera hablar con...
kees-yerra ablar kon...

I have an appointment with...

Tengo una cita con...
tengo oona theeta kon...

...the director

...el director/la directora
el dirrektor/la dirrektora

...the manager

...el/la gerente
el/la herrenteh

...the personnel manager

...el jefe/la jefa de personal
el hefeh/la heffa deh pairsonal

...the sales manager

...el jefe/la jefa de ventas
el hefeh/la heffa deh bentas

I need...

Necesito...
netheseeto...

...a secretary

...un secretario/una secretaria
oon sekretaryo/oona sekretarya

...an interpreter

...un/una intérprete
oon/oona eentairpreteh

...a translator

...un traductor/una traductora
oon tradooktor/oona tradooktora

Can you...?

¿Puede...?
pwedeh...?

...cancel my appointment with...

...cancelar mi cita con...
kanthelar mee theeta kon...

...make another appointment

...fijar otra cita
fee-har otra theeta

• For other business expressions, see page 70.

AT THE POST OFFICE

• Look for the sign *Correos*.

• There is no need to go to a post office if you only want to buy stamps. Buy these in a tobacconist's (*Estanco*).

• Post offices are normally open from 8.30am to 2pm although times will vary depending on the size of the town or city and the area you are visiting. Most post offices also open on Saturday mornings.

• The different sections are found under the following signs: *Certificados* (recorded delivery), *Venta de Sellos* (stamps), *Paquetes* (parcels), *Giros* (if you wish to cash a National Girobank Postcheque on your own post office account or send money).

• You can also send faxes from most post offices.

• If you wish to receive *poste restante* mail, the sender should address the letter with your name, *Lista de Correos*, the name of the town or village, the name of the province, and the post code.

• If you have to collect a registered letter or package, make sure you have your passport as ID.

A stamp for England/the United States	Un sello para Inglaterra/ Estados Unidos *oon seh-yo para inglaterra/ estados ooneedos*
Two (75 cent) stamps	Dos sellos (de setenta y cinco céntimos) *dos seh-yos (deh setenta-ee- theenko thenteemos)*
I'd like to send...	Quiero mandar... *kee-yerro mandar...*

You can also send faxes from most post offices.

...this letter	...esta carta *esta karta*
...this parcel	...este paquete *esteh paketteh*
...this postcard	...esta postal *esta postal*
by airmail	por avión *por ab-yon*
by surface mail	por correo normal *por koreyo normal*
first class	urgente *oorhenteh*
by recorded delivery	certificado/a *thairteefeekado/a*
Is there a giro/parcel for me?	¿Hay un giro/un paquete para mí? *I oon heero/oon paketteh para mee?*
I'd like a post office box	Quiero un apartado de correos *kee-yerro oon apartado deh koreos*
I'd like to send a giro/a telegram to this address	Quiero mandar un giro/ poner un telegrama a esta dirección *kee-yerro mandar oon heero/ ponair oon telegrama a esta deerekth-yon*
How much does it cost per word?	¿Cuánto cuesta por palabra? *kwanto kwesta por palabra?*
How long will it take to arrive?	¿Cuánto tardará en llegar? *kwanto tardara en yeggar?*

You may hear:

Vaya a aquella ventanilla
baya a akehya bentaneeya

Please go to that window

Rellene este impreso/formulario
reyenneh esteh eempreso/formoolar-yo

Please fill in this form

Ponga la dirección aquí
ponga la deerekth-yon akee

Please put the address here

No puede enviarlo así
no pwedeh enbee-yarlo asee

You can't send it like that

TELEPHONING

- Telephone boxes have clear displays of international phone codes and operating instructions in a number of languages including English.

- To phone the UK, dial 0044 plus the remaining code without the initial 0.

- In many of the larger towns and tourist resorts you will find telephone call centres offering cheap-rate international calls. You make your call from a booth and pay at the desk.

- If you phone from a hotel you will be charged extra.

- There are often public phones in bars, but these cost more to use.

- Phone cards (*tarjetas telefónicas*) are available from *estancos* and post offices.

- Some public phones only accept cards and not coins or you may find the coin slot is broken, so a phone card is useful to have.

If you have to collect a registered letter or package, make sure you have your passport as ID.

- Some telephone companies sell discount telephone cards, which can be bought from various retail outlets. These cards are not inserted into a slot but have a code number or PIN which you key in after you have phoned a Freephone number.

- If you have a mobile phone which operates in Europe, you will receive a message from the local service provider when you arrive and its name will appear on your LED. This may be *Airtel* or *Movistar*, or others, depending on which one operates in your area. This may change as you move around. Using your mobile phone is very convenient but can be expensive on long calls. You will also be charged by the service provider for receiving incoming calls.

- You can also buy contract-free mobile phones in Spain, which you buy inclusive of a certain number of calls. If you plan to spend some time in Spain and have to call people locally, this may be worthwhile. Note that all Spanish mobile phone numbers begin with 6.

- Inland phone numbers in Spain have nine digits and all begin with a 9, which is part of the area dialling code. For example the code for Madrid is 91 and for Barcelona 93. You must use this code even if you are dialling a local number.

- Note the following special numbers: numbers beginning with 900 are freephone numbers, 901 numbers are charged at a local call rate, 902 at the national call rate, 906 at the premium rate (chat lines etc.).

Is there a phone box near here?	¿Hay una cabina por aquí?
	I oona kabeena por akee?

Some public phones only accept cards and not coins or you may find the coin slot is broken, so a phone card is useful to have.

Can I use the phone?	¿Puedo usar el teléfono? *pwedo oosar el telefono?*
Where is the phone?	¿Dónde está el teléfono? *dondeh esta el telefono?*
Do you have the phone book?	¿Tiene la guía telefónica? *tee-yenneh la geea telefonikka?*
What is the code for (London)?	¿Qué prefijo es para (Londres)? *keh prehfee-ho es para (londres)?*
Can I speak to...?	¿Puedo hablar con...? *pwedo ablar kon...?*
Could I have extension...	Quiero la extensión... *kee-yerro la extens-yon...*
I'll call back later	Llamaré más tarde *yamareh mas tardeh*
It's (Mrs Smith) (informal)	Soy (la señora Smith) *soy (la senyora smeeth)*
It's (Miss Smith) (formal)	De parte de (la señorita Smith) *deh parteh deh (la senyoreeta smeeth)*
Can I leave a message?	¿Puedo dejar un recado? *pwedo deh-har oon rekado?*
Can you ask him/her to call me?	¿Puede decirle que me llame? *pwedeh detheerleh keh meh yameh?*
My number is...	Mi número es... *mee noomero es...*
I'm sorry, I've got the wrong number	Perdone, me he equivocado de número *pairdoneh, meh eh ekeebokado deh noomero*

 Inland phone numbers in Spain have nine digits and all begin with a 9, which is part of the area dialling code. For example the code for Madrid is 91 and for Barcelona 93. You must use this code even if you are dialling a local number.

TALKING TO THE OPERATOR

Could you...?	¿Puede...?
	pwedeh...?
...give me Mr Smith's number	...darme el número del señor Smith
	darmeh el noomero del senyor smeeth
...tell me the cost of the call	...decirme cuánto es la llamada
	detheermeh kwanto es la yamada
I've been cut off	Se ha cortado la línea
	seh a kortado la leenya
Can I pay by card?	¿Puedo pagar con tarjeta?
	pwedo pagar kon tarhetta?
I'd like to reverse the charges/ I'd like to make a collect call	Quiero llamar a cobro revertido
	kee-yerro yamar a kobro rebairteedo

ANSWERING THE PHONE

Hello	Dígame
	deegameh
It's me	Soy yo
	soy yo
One moment, please	Un momento, por favor
	oon momento, por fabbor

You may hear:

Dígame	Hello
deegameh	
Hay una llamada para usted	There is a call for you
I oona yamada para oosted	
¿Quiere dejar un recado?	Would you like to leave a message?
kee-yerreh deh-har oon rekado?	

Se ha equivocado de número *seh a ekeebokado deh noomero*	You have the wrong number
¿Cuál es su número? *kwal es soo noomero?*	What's your number?
No cuelgue *no kwelgeh*	Don't hang up
No contesta *no kontesta*	There is no answer
Comunica/está comunicando *komooneeka/esta komooneekando*	It's engaged
Hable *ableh*	Speak now, please
Las líneas están ocupadas *las leenyas estan okoopadas*	The lines are busy
Espere, por favor *esperreh, por fabbor*	Can you hold, please?
Lo intentaré otra vez *lo intentareh otra beth*	I'll try again

USING THE INTERNET

- Most towns and cities in Spain now offer Internet facilities. These may form part of the public telephone call centres already mentioned, or may be solely dedicated to Internet use. You may also find cafeterias (*cibercafé*) which offer the service. There are various methods of payment, based on the time you are connected.

I would like	Quiero *kee-yerro*
...to use a computer	...usar un ordenador *oosar oon ordenador*
...to use the Internet	...usar internet *oosar intairnet*

...send an email

...enviar un email
enbee-ar oon eemail

How much is it?

¿Cuánto cuesta?
kwanto kwesta?

POLICE

- There are three separate police forces in Spain, each with their own distinctive uniforms and each with different, clearly defined duties.

- The local or Municipal Police (*Policía Municipal*) wear blue and white uniforms and are mainly responsible for traffic police duties. They are also most likely to help tourists as they are representative of their town.

- The duties of the National Police force (*Policía Nacional*) include crime investigation, personnel protection and guarding of public buildings. They are most evident in the larger cities. You may see them in a black uniform or a blue military style uniform. If you need to find a police station, look for the sign *Comisaría*.

- The Civil Guard (*Guardia Civil*) wear green uniforms and are responsible for law and order and traffic in more rural areas and in small towns. If you have any problems on the open road, you will deal with the *Guardia Civil*.

- If you lose your passport or are the victim of a robbery or other crime, you must go to the nearest *Comisaría* and make a statement (*una denuncia*). The police will issue you with a copy of the statement for your consulate, your insurance company or your bank if your credit card has been taken and used.

- If you need a residence or work permit you also need to make enquiries at a police station.

If you need to find a police station, look for the sign *Comisaría*.

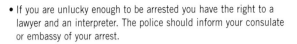
- If you are unlucky enough to be arrested you have the right to a lawyer and an interpreter. The police should inform your consulate or embassy of your arrest.

- Ask at the airport or in the tourist office for a brochure produced by the police in different languages on safety and security for tourists.

- Lost property should find its way to the lost property office (*Oficina de Objetos Perdidos*) in the town hall (*Ayuntamiento*).

- If you require a special visa or work permit, obtain these in advance from the Spanish Consulate, 20 Draycott Place, London SW3 2RZ.

My son/daughter is lost	Mi hijo/hija se ha perdido *mee ee-ho/ee-ha seh a pairdeedo*
My friend has disappeared	Mi amigo/a ha desaparecido *mee ameego/a a desaparetheedo*
I've lost...	He perdido... *eh pairdeedo...*
Someone has stolen...	Me han robado... *meh an robado...*
...my camera	...la cámara *la kamara*
...my car	...el coche *el kocheh*
...my car radio	...la radio del coche *la radyo del kocheh*
...my jewels	...las joyas *las hoyas*

Ask at the airport or in the tourist office for a brochure produced by the police in different languages on safety and security for tourists.

...my luggage	...el equipaje *el ekeepaheh*
...my money	...el dinero *el dinerro*
...my purse	...el monedero *el monederro*
...my wallet	...la cartera *la karterra*
...my airline tickets	...los billetes de avión *los beeyetes deh ab-yon*
...my (car) keys	...las llaves (del coche) *las yabbes del kocheh*
...my driving licence	...el carnet de conducir *el karnay deh kondootheer*
...my watch	...el reloj *el reloh*
I left it in the hotel/taxi	Lo he dejado en el hotel/en un taxi *lo eh de-hado en el otel/en oon taxee*
It happened...	Ha sido... *a seedo...*
...a moment ago	...hace un momento *atheh oon momento*
...this morning	...esta mañana *esta man-yana*
...in the underground	...en el metro *en el metro*
...in the street	...en la calle *en la ka-yeh*
It was a man/woman	Fue un hombre/una mujer *fweh oon ombreh/oona moohair*
I don't know who it was	No sé quién fue *no seh kee-yen fweh*

I don't know...it happened	No sé...fue
	no seh...fweh
...when	...cuándo
	kwando
...where	...dónde
	dondeh
...how	...cómo
	komo

• For other expressions of time, see page 147.

DESCRIPTIONS

tall	alto/a
	alto/a
short	bajo/a
	baho/a
medium height	mediano/a
	med-yano/a
fat	gordo/a
	gordo/a
thin	delgado/a
	delgado/a
dark	moreno/a
	morenno/a
blonde	rubio/a
	roob-yo/a
red haired	pelirrojo/a
	pelee-roho/a
with...eyes	de ojos...
	deh ohos...
...blue	...azules
	athool-es
...green	...verdes
	baird-es

...brown	...castaños *kastanyos*
...dark	...negros *neggros*
with...hair	de pelo... *deh pelo...*
...short	...corto *korto*
...long	...largo *largo*
...straight	...liso *leeso*
...curly	...rizado *reethado*
bearded	con barba *kon barba*
with a moustache	con bigote *kon beegoteh*
(slightly) bald	(un poco) calvo *(oon poko) kalbo*
He/she was wearing...	Llevaba... *yebaba...*
...glasses	...gafas *gafas*
...a blue jersey	...jersey azul *hairseh athool*
I'm lost	Me he perdido *meh eh pairdeedo*
Could you call the British Consulate?	Por favor, llame al Consulado Británico *por fabbor, yameh al konsoolado britanikko*

You may hear:

Deme los datos, por favor *demeh los dattos, por fabbor*	Could you give me all the details
¿Cómo es? *komo es?*	What is he/she/it like?
¿Cuándo...? *kwando...?*	When...?
¿Dónde...? *dondeh...?*	Where...?
¿Cómo...? *komo...?*	How...?
¿Quién...? *kee-yen...?*	Who...?
...fue/ha sido *fweh/a seedo*	...was it
Aquí no está *akee no esta*	It's not here
Le avisaremos *leh abeesaremmos*	We'll let you know

• For giving personal details, see page 65.

ESSENTIAL INFORMATION

CARDINAL NUMBERS

0	cero *thairro*		15	quince *keentheh*
1	uno *oono*		16	dieciséis *dee-yethee-seys*
2	dos *dos*		17	diecisiete *dee-yethee-see-yeteh*
3	tres *tres*		18	dieciocho *dee-yethee-ocho*
4	cuatro *kwatro*		19	diecinueve *dee-yethee-nwebbeh*
5	cinco *theenko*		20	veinte *beynteh*
6	seis *seys*		21	veintiuno *beyntee-oono*
7	siete *see-yeteh*		30	treinta *treynta*
8	ocho *ocho*		40	cuarenta *kwarenta*
9	nueve *nwebbeh*		50	cincuenta *thinkwenta*
10	diez *dee-yeth*		60	sesenta *sesenta*
11	once *ontheh*		70	setenta *setenta*
12	doce *dotheh*		80	ochenta *ochenta*
13	trece *tretheh*		90	noventa *nobenta*
14	catorce *katortheh*		100	cien *thee-yen*

ORDINAL NUMBERS

1st	primero	*preemero*
2nd	segundo	*segoondo*
3rd	tercero	*tairthero*
4th	cuarto	*kwarto*
5th	quinto	*keento*
6th	sexto	*sexto*

DAYS OF THE WEEK

Monday	lunes	*loon-es*
Tuesday	martes	*mart-es*
Wednesday	miércoles	*mee-yairkol-es*
Thursday	jueves	*hweb-es*
Friday	viernes	*bee-yairn-es*
Saturday	sábado	*sabaddo*
Sunday	domingo	*domeengo*

MONTHS

January	enero	*enerro*
February	febrero	*febrerro*
March	marzo	*martho*
April	abril	*abreel*
May	mayo	*mI-o*
June	junio	*hoonyo*
July	julio	*hoolyo*
August	agosto	*agosto*
September	septiembre	*set-yembreh*
October	octubre	*oktoobreh*
November	noviembre	*nob-yembreh*
December	diciembre	*deeth-yembreh*

PUBLIC HOLIDAYS

January 1st	Año Nuevo	New Year's Day
January 6th	Día de Reyes (Epifanía)	Epiphany
March 19th	San José	St Joseph's Day
March or April	Jueves Santo	Maundy Thursday
	Viernes Santo	Good Friday
	Semana Santa	Easter
May 1st	Día del Trabajo	Labour Day
July 25th	Día de Santiago	St James's Day
August 15th	La Asunción	Assumption Day
October 12th	Día de La Hispanidad (Día del Pilar)	Columbus Day
November 1st	Día de Todos los Santos	All Saints' Day
December 6th	Día de La Constitución	Constitution Day
December 8th	La Inmaculada Concepción	Immaculate Conception
December 25th	Día de Navidad	Christmas Day

COLOURS

black	negro/a *neggro/a*	pink	rosa *rosa*
blue	azul *athool*	red	rojo/a *roho/a*
brown	marrón *marron*	white	blanco/a *blanko/a*
green	verde *bairdeh*	yellow	amarillo/a *amareeyo/a*
grey	gris *grees*	orange	naranja *naranha*

TIMES AND DAYS

What time is it?	¿Qué hora es? *keh ora es?*
It's one o'clock	Es la una *es la oona*
It's two o'clock	Son las dos *son las dos*
It's a quarter past three	Son las tres y cuarto *son las tres ee kwarto*
It's twenty to eleven	Son las once menos veinte *son las ontheh menos beynteh*
...am	...de la mañana *deh la man-yana*
...pm (afternoon/evening)	...de la tarde *deh la tardeh*
...pm (evening/night)	...de la noche *deh la nocheh*
midday	mediodía *med-yodeea*
midnight	medianoche *med-yanocheh*
At what time...?	¿A qué hora...? *a keh ora...?*
At six o'clock	A las seis *a las seys*
In five minutes	En cinco minutos *en theenko minootos*
Half an hour ago	Hace media hora *atheh med-ya ora*
today	hoy *oy*
yesterday	ayer *ayair*

tomorrow	mañana *man-yana*
in the morning	por la mañana *por la man-yana*
in the afternoon/evening	por la tarde *por la tardeh*
at night	por la noche *por la nocheh*
last night	anoche *anocheh*
this morning	esta mañana *esta man-yana*
this afternoon/evening	esta tarde *esta tardeh*
tonight	esta noche *esta nocheh*
the day before yesterday	anteayer *anteh-lair*
the day after tomorrow	pasado mañana *pasado man-yana*
next week	la semana que viene *la semana keh bee-yenneh*
next Monday	el lunes próximo *el loon-es proxeemo*
last Monday	el lunes pasado *el loon-es pasado*
on Monday	el lunes *el loon-es*
on Mondays	los lunes *los loon-es*
before	antes *ant-es*

after	**después** *despwes*
until	**hasta** *asta*
during	**durante** *dooranteh*
(at) the beginning...	**(a) principios...** *(a) preentheep-yos...*
(in) the middle...	**(a) mediados...** *(a) med-yados...*
(at) the end...	**(a) finales...** *(a) feenal-es...*
...of August	**...de agosto** *deh agosto*
What's the date today?	**¿A qué fecha estamos?** *a keh fecha estamos?*
It's...	**Es...** *es...*
...the 1st of May	**...el uno de mayo** *el oono deh mÍ-o*
...the 5th of April	**...el cinco de abril** *el theenko deh abreel*

SEASONS

Spring	**primavera** *preemaberra*
Summer	**verano** *berano*
Autumn	**otoño** *otonyo*
Winter	**invierno** *eenbee-yerno*

CLOTHES SIZES

Note that sizes vary from brand to brand and from style to style, so any comparison must be taken as approximate only.

Men's jackets

British	34	36	38	40	42	44	46	48
European	44	46	48	50	52	54	56	58

Men's shirts

British	14	$14\frac{1}{2}$	15	$15\frac{1}{2}$	16	$16\frac{1}{2}$	17	$17\frac{1}{2}$
European	36	37	38	39	41	42	43	44

Men's shoes

British	$5\frac{1}{2}$	$6\frac{1}{2}$	$7\frac{1}{2}$	$8\frac{1}{2}$	$9\frac{1}{2}$	$10\frac{1}{2}$	$11\frac{1}{2}$	$12\frac{1}{2}$
European	38	39	40	41	42	43	44	45

Women's dresses

British	8	10	12	14	16	18	20
European	36	38	40	42	44	46	48

Women's shoes

British	$2\frac{1}{2}$	$3\frac{1}{2}$	$4\frac{1}{2}$	$5\frac{1}{2}$	$6\frac{1}{2}$	$7\frac{1}{2}$	$8\frac{1}{2}$
European	36	37	38	39	40	41	42

MATERIALS

brass	latón	*laton*
glass	cristal	*kreestal*
metal	de metal	*deh metal*
wooden	de madera	*deh maderra*

PATTERNS AND FABRICS

plain	liso/a	*leeso/a*
printed	estampado/a	*estampado/a*
striped	a rayas	*a r-I-as*
checked	a cuadros	*a kwadros*
dotted	de lunares	*deh loonar-es*
satin	raso	*raso*

ABBREVIATIONS

C	caliente	hot water (tap)
dcha	derecha	right
F	fría	cold water (tap)
IVA	impuesto del valor añadido	VAT
izq	izquierda	left
PVP	precio de venta al público	retail price
RENFE	Red Nacional de Ferrocarriles Españoles	Spanish railway company
SR	sin reserva	unreserved

SIGNS AND PUBLIC NOTICES

abierto	open
agua potable	drinking water
aseos	toilets
centro ciudad	town centre
cerrado (por vacaciones)	closed (for holidays)
empujar	push
Entrada	Way in
horario (de verano)	(summer) timetable
libre	vacant
no tocar	do not touch
ocupado	occupied
parada solicitada	request stop
peligro	danger
prohibido	prohibited
prohibido fumar	no smoking
prohibido el paso	no trespassing
prohibido pisar el césped	keep off the grass
recién pintado	wet paint
recoja el ticket	take a ticket
Salida	Way out
se prohíbe la entrada	no entry/no admission
tirar	pull

DICTIONARY

Both masculine and feminine forms are given for adjectives
eg. alone: solo/a = solo (m)/sola (f).

A
a un/una
abdomen el abdomen
to be able poder
about aproximadamente/
    más o menos
above encima (de)
abroad al extranjero
abcess el flemón
accelerator el acelerador
to accept aceptar
accident el accidente
accommodation el alojamiento
account la cuenta
ache el dolor
to ache doler
across a través (de)/al otro lado
activity la actividad
actor el actor
actress la actriz
adaptor el adaptador
address la dirección
adhesive tape la cinta adhesiva
admission la entrada
to admit admitir
adult adulto/a
advance (cash) el anticipo
advertisement el anuncio

aerial la antena
aeroplane el avión
Africa África
African africano/a
after después (de)
afternoon la tarde
aftershave la loción de afeitar
again otra vez
age la edad
agent agente/
    representante (m/f)
to agree estar de acuerdo
air conditioning el aire
    acondicionado
airline la línea aérea
airmail el correo aéreo
airport el aeropuerto
alarm clock el despertador
alcohol el alcohol
all todo/a
allergic alérgico/a
allergy la alergia
alone solo/a
already ya
also también
although aunque
always siempre
amazing asombroso/a

ambulance la ambulancia
America Estados Unidos
American americano/a
amount la cantidad
amusing divertido/a
anaesthetic el anestésico
and y
angry enfadado/a
animal el animal
ankle el tobillo
annoyed enfadado/a
anorak el anorak
another otro/a
answer la respuesta
antibiotic el antibiótico
antidote el antídoto
antifreeze el anticongelante
antique la antigüedad
antiseptic el antiséptico
anxious preocupado/a
any alguno/a; ninguno/a
apartment el apartamento
apology la disculpa
appendicitis la apendicitis
apple la manzana
appointment la cita
approximately aproximadamente
apricot el albaricoque
architect el arquitecto/la
    arquitecta
area (la) área
area code el código/
    el prefijo
arm el brazo
armchair el sillón
around alrededor (de)

to arrive llegar
arrival la llegada
art el arte
art gallery la galería de arte
artichoke la alcachofa
artist el/la artista
ashtray el cenicero
to ask pedir/preguntar/invitar
asleep dormido/a
asparagus el espárrago
aspirin la aspirina
assistant el/la ayudante
asthma (la) asma
at a/en
atmosphere el ambiente
attack el ataque
attention la atención
attic el desván
attractive atractivo/a
aubergine la berenjena
aunt la tía
Australia Australia
Australian australiano/a
automatic automático/a
autumn el otoño
avocado el aguacate
away fuera/lejos (de)
awful horrible

B
baby el/la bebé
babysitter la niñera
back la espalda
backache el dolor de espalda
bacon el tocino
bad malo/a

bag bolsa
  (hand)bag bolso
baggage el equipaje
bakery la panadería
balcony el balcón
  (theatre) el anfiteatro
ball (dance) el baile
  (toy) la pelota
ball-point pen el bolígrafo
ban la prohibición
to ban prohibir
banana el plátano
band el grupo/la orquesta
bandage la venda
bank holiday el día festivo
banknote el billete
bar (pub) el bar
bar (rod/chocolate) la barra
barbecue la barbacoa
barber's shop la barbería
basement el sótano
basket la cesta
basketball el baloncesto
bath el baño
to bathe bañarse
bathing cap el gorro de baño
bathrobe el albornoz
bathroom el cuarto de baño
battery (small) la pila
  (car) la batería
bay la bahía
to be ser/estar
beach la playa
bean la judía
beard la barba
beautiful hermoso/a

beauty salon el salón de
  belleza
because porque
bed la cama
bedding la ropa de cama
bedroom el dormitorio
bee la abeja
beef la carne de vaca
beer la cerveza
beetroot la remolacha
before antes (de)
to begin empezar/comenzar
beginner el/la principiante
behind atrás (de)/detrás (de)
bell el timbre/la campana
below abajo/debajo (de)
belt el cinturón
bench el banco
bend (in the road) la curva
best el/la mejor
better mejor
between entre
bib el babero
bicycle la bicicleta
big grande
bikini el bikini
bill la cuenta
bin la papelera/el cubo de
  basura
binoculars los prismáticos
bird el pájaro
birthday el cumpleaños
biscuit la galleta
bite la picadura
to bite morder/(insect) picar
bitter amargo/a

black negro/a
black pudding la morcilla
blanket la manta
bleach la lejía
bleeding la hemorragia
blind (for a window) la persiana
  (can't see) ciego/a
blister la ampolla
blonde rubio/a
blood la sangre
blood pressure la tensión
blouse la blusa
blue azul
boat el barco/la barca
body el cuerpo
boiled hervido/a
boiled egg (soft) el huevo
  pasado por agua
  (hard) el huevo duro
bone el hueso
book el libro
to book reservar
booking office
  (theatre) la taquilla
  (rail) el despacho de billetes
bookshop la librería
boot (shoe) la bota
  (car) el capó
border la frontera
boring aburrido/a
both ambos/as/los/las dos
bottle la botella
bottle-opener el abridor de
  botellas
box la caja
box office la taquilla

boy el niño/el chico
boyfriend el amigo/el novio
bra el sujetador
bracelet la pulsera
brakes los frenos
brake fluid el líquido de
  frenos
brand la marca
brandy el coñac
bread el pan
to break romper
breakdown (car) la avería
breakdown lorry la grúa
breakfast el desayuno
breast el pecho
to breathe respirar
bridge el puente
briefcase la cartera
to bring traer
Britain Gran Bretaña
British británico/a
broken roto/a
brochure el folleto
broom la escoba
brother el hermano
brother-in-law el cuñado
brown (colour) marrón
  (hair/eyes) castaño/a
  (tan) moreno/a
bruise la contusión/la
  moradura
brush el cepillo
bucket el cubo
building el edificio
bulb la bombilla
bull el toro

bullfight la corrida
bullfighter el torero
bullring la plaza de toros
bump el golpe
bumper el parachoques
bunch (of flowers) el ramo
bungalow el bungalow
bunk la litera
burglar el ladrón/la ladrona
burglary el robo
burn la quemadura
to burn quemar
bus el autobús
bus station la estación de
  autobuses
bus stop la parada
business el negocio
business trip el viaje de
  negocios
but pero
butcher's shop la carnicería
butter la mantequilla
button el botón
to buy comprar

C
cab el taxi
cabbage el repollo
cabin crew member el/la
  auxiliar de vuelo
cafe la cafetería
cake el pastel, la tarta
cake shop la pastelería
calendar el calendario
call (telephone) la llamada
to call (shout) llamar

  (telephone) telefonear
camera la cámara fotográfica
camp el campamento
to camp acampar/hacer
  camping
camp site el camping
can (to be able) poder
can la lata
Canada Canadá
Canadian canadiense
to cancel cancelar/anular
candy el caramelo
can opener el abrelatas
car el coche
caravan la caravana
carburettor el carburador
card (visiting) la tarjeta
  (postcard) la postal
  (membership) el carnet
cardigan la chaqueta de punto
careful! ¡cuidado!
car hire el alquiler de coches
car park el parking/
  el aparcamiento
carriage el vagón/el coche
carrot la zanahoria
to carry llevar
carton (of cigarettes) el cartón
  (de cigarrillos)
car wash el lavado de coches
case (for jewels, glasses)
  el estuche
  (suitcase) la maleta
cash el dinero
to cash cobrar
cash desk la caja

cashier cajero/a

cassette el cassette/la cinta

castanets las castañuelas

castle el castillo

cat el gato

cathedral la catedral

cauliflower la coliflor

celery el apio

cellar la bodega

central heating la calefacción central

centre el centro

century el siglo

ceramics la cerámica

chain la cadena

chair la silla

chalet el chalet

champagne (French)
el champán
(Spanish) el cava

change el cambio

to change cambiar

changing room el probador

chapel la capilla

to charge cobrar

charter flight el vuelo charter

cheap barato/a

to check revisar/comprobar

to check in (hotel) inscribirse
(airport) presentarse

checkup (medical)
el reconocimiento

cheerio! ¡hasta luego!

cheers! ¡salud!

cheese el queso

chemist's la farmacia

cheque el cheque

chequebook el talonario

cheque card la tarjeta de banco

cherry la cereza

chest el pecho

chewing gum el chicle

chicken el pollo

chicken breast la pechuga de pollo

chick pea el garbanzo

child el niño/la niña

China China

china la porcelana

Chinese chino/a

chips las patatas fritas

chlorine el cloro

chocolate el chocolate

chop la chuleta

Christmas la Navidad

church la iglesia

cider la sidra

cigar el puro

cigarette el cigarrillo

cigarette lighter el encendedor

cigarette paper el papel de fumar

cinema el cine

circle (theatre) el anfiteatro
(shape) el círculo

circus el circo

city la ciudad

civil servant funcionario/a

claim la reclamación

to claim reclamar

class la clase

clean limpio/a

to clean limpiar
client el/la cliente
climate el clima
clinic la clínica
cloakroom el guardarropa
clock (wall) el reloj
  (alarm) el despertador
to close cerrar
closed cerrado/a
cloth la tela
clothes la ropa
cloud la nube
club el club
clutch (car) el embrague
coach el autocar
coast la costa
coat el abrigo
cocoa el cacao
coconut el coco
code el código
  (area) code el prefijo
coffee el café
  (black) el café solo
  (white) el café con leche
coin la moneda
cold el frío
to be cold (person) tener frío
  (weather) hacer frío
to have a cold estar resfriado/a
collar el cuello
colour el color
comb el peine
to come venir
comedy la comedia
comfortable cómodo/a
comic (magazine) el tebeo

Common Market Mercado el Común
compact disc el disco compacto
company la compañía/la empresa
to complain quejarse
complaint la queja
computer el ordenador/ la computadora
concert el concierto
concussion la conmoción cerebral
condom el preservativo
conductor (bus) el cobrador/ la cobradora
confectioner's la confitería
congratulations las felicidades
connection (transport) la conexión/el transbordo
constipated estreñido/a
consulate el consulado
contact lens la lente de contacto
contagious contagioso/a
contraceptive el anticonceptivo
control el control
controller el controlador
cooker la cocina
cool fresco/a
cork el corcho
corkscrew el sacacorchos
corn el maíz
corner la esquina
cosmetics los cosméticos
cost el precio
to cost costar
costume el traje

cot la cuna
cottage el chalet
cottage cheese el requesón
cotton el algodón
cotton wool el algodón
cough la tos
to cough toser
counter (shop) el mostrador
country el país
countryside el campo
couple la pareja
courgette el calabacín
course (meal) el plato
  (golf) el campo
cousin el primo/la prima
crab el cangrejo
crafts la artesanía
cramp el calambre
crash el choque
crash course el curso intensivo
crash helmet el casco
cream la nata
credit card la tarjeta de crédito
crisps las patatas fritas
crossing el cruce
  (pedestrian) el paso de
  peatones
crossroads el cruce
cruise el crucero
cucumber el pepino
cuisine la cocina
cup la taza
to cure curar
currency la moneda
current la corriente
current account la cuenta
  corriente
cushion el cojín
custard la natilla
customs la aduana
customer el/la cliente
cut el corte
  (wound) la herida
to cut cortar
cutlery los cubiertos
cycling el ciclismo
cyclist el/la ciclista

D

daily diariamente
dairy la lechería
dance el baile
to dance bailar
dance hall la sala de baile
danger el peligro
dangerous peligroso/a
dark oscuro/a
date (calendar) la fecha
  (fruit) el dátil
daughter la hija
day el día
deaf sordo/a
dear querido/a
dear Sir/Madam
  (letter) estimado/a
  señor/señora
deck chair la hamaca
deep profundo/a
to dehydrate deshidratar
delay el retraso
delicate delicado/a
delicatessen la mantequería

delivery service el servicio a domicilio

dentist el/la dentista

denture la dentadura postiza

deodorant el desodorante

department el departamento

department store los grandes almacenes

deposit el depósito

to deposit (bank) ingresar

dessert el postre

detergent el detergente

detour el desvío

diabetes la diabetes

diabetic diabético/a

to dial marcar

dialling tone la señal de marcar

diarrhoea la diarrea

dictionary el diccionario

diesel oil el gasoil

diet el régimen

difficult difícil

dining-car el coche restaurante

dining-room el comedor

dinner la cena

dinner jacket el esmoquin

direct directo/a

direction la dirección

directions las instrucciones

directory el listín

(telephone) directory la guía telefónica

dirty sucio/a

disabled discapacitado/a

discount el descuento

dish el plato

dishwasher el lavaplatos /el lavavajillas

disinfectant el desinfectante

distance la distancia

to disturb molestar

diversion el desvío

divorced divorciado/a

dizzy mareado/a

doctor el médico/la médica

dog el perro

do-it-yourself el bricolaje

doll la muñeca

dollar el dólar

door la puerta

doorbell el timbre

double doble

double bed la cama de matrimonio/la cama doble

double room la habitación doble

down abajo

downstairs abajo

dozen la docena

drawer el cajón

dress el vestido

(evening) dress el traje de noche

dressing gown la bata

drier el secador

drink la bebida

to drink beber

drinking water (la) agua potable

to drive conducir

driving licence el permiso de conducir

drug el medicamento

drugs las drogas
drunk borracho/a
dry seco/a
to dry clean limpiar en seco
dry cleaner's la tintorería
dual carriageway la carretera de doble carril
dummy (baby) el chupete
during durante
duty (tax) los impuestos
duty-free libre de impuestos

E
each cada
ear la oreja
earache el dolor de oído
early temprano/pronto
earring el pendiente
easy fácil
to eat comer
eczema el eczema
egg el huevo
elbow el codo
electric eléctrico/a
electrician el/la electricista
electricity la electricidad
embassy la embajada
emergency la emergencia /la urgencia
emergency exit la salida de emergencia
employer el/la empresario/a
empty vacío/a
end la final
engine el motor
England Inglaterra

English inglés/esa
to enjoy oneself divertirse
enjoyable divertido/a
enough bastante
to enrol (school) matricularse
entertaining entretenido/a
entrance la entrada
envelope el sobre
environment el ambiente
epilepsy la epilepsia
equipment el equipo
error el error
escalator la escalera mecánica
evening (early) la tarde (late) la noche
exactly exactamente
exchange rate el cambio
excursion la excursión
excuse me! ¡oiga!/perdone
exercise el ejercicio
exhaust pipe el tubo de escape
exhibition la exposición
exit la salida
expenses los gastos
expensive caro/a
to export exportar
express (delivery) urgente (train) el rápido
extension (telephone) la extensión
eye el ojo
eye drops las gotas para los ojos
eye shadow la sombra de ojos
eye specialist el/la oculista

eye witness el/la testigo

F
fabric el tejido
face la cara
factory la fábrica
to faint desmayarse
fair (hair) rubio/a
    (funfair) la feria/el parque de
    atracciones
fall la caída
to fall caerse
family la familia
fan (hand) el abanico
    (electric) el ventilador
    (sports) aficionado/a
fanbelt la correa del ventilador
fancy dress el disfraz
far lejos
fare el precio del billete
farm la granja
fashion la moda
fast rápido/a
to fasten abrochar
fat (meat) la grasa
    (person) gordo/a
father el padre
fault (person) la culpa
    (object) el defecto
to fax mandar un fax
fee el precio
feeding bottle el biberón
to feel (ill) sentirse (mal)
    (touch) tocar
ferry el transbordador
fever la fiebre

few pocos/as
field el campo
fig el higo
to fill llenar
filling (tooth) el empaste
filling station la gasolinera
film (cinema) la película
    (photo) el rollo
filter el filtro
fine! ¡muy bien!
finger el dedo
to finish terminar
fire el fuego
    (gas or electric) la estufa
fire alarm la alarma de
    incendios
fire brigade los bomberos
fire escape la escalera de
    incendios
fire extinguisher el extintor
fireplace la chimenea
fireproof incombustible
firm (business) la empresa
first aid los primeros auxilios
first name el nombre (de pila)
fish el pescado
to fish pescar
fishbone la espina
fishmonger's la pescadería
fitting room el probador
flashlight la linterna
flat llano/a, plano/a
    (battery) la batería descargada
    (apartment) el piso
flat tyre el pinchazo
flight el vuelo

flip-flops las chancletas
floor (ground) el suelo
  (in building) el piso
florist's la floristería
flour la harina
flower la flor
flu la gripe
fly la mosca
to fly volar
fog la niebla
folding plegable
food la comida
food poisoning la intoxicación
  alimenticia
foot el pie
football el fútbol
footpath el camino
for por/para
forbidden prohibido/a
forecast (weather) el
  pronóstico del tiempo
forehead la frente
foreign extranjero/a
forest el bosque
fork el tenedor
form (shape) la forma
  (document) la ficha
fortnight quince días
  /la quincena
fountain la fuente
fracture la fractura
fragile frágil
France Francia
free (vacant) libre
  (no charge) gratis
French francés/esa

frequent frecuente
fresh fresco/a
fridge la nevera/el frigorífico
fried frito/a
friend amigo/a
friendly simpático/a
from de/desde
front la parte delantera
frontier la frontera
frozen congelado/a
fruit la fruta
fruit machine la máquina
  tragaperras
fruit juice el zumo de fruta
  /el jugo
fruit salad la macedonia de
  frutas
fruit shop la frutería
to fry freír
frying pan la sartén
full lleno/a
full board la pensión completa
full insurance el seguro a todo
  riesgo
funfair la feria /el parque de
  atracciones
funny (comic) divertido/a
  (strange) extraño/a
furnished amueblado/a
furniture los muebles
further más lejos/más allá
fuse el fusible
fuse box la caja de fusibles

G

game el juego
garage el garaje
garden el jardín
garlic el ajo
gas el gas
gate la puerta
gear (car) la marcha
gearbox la caja de velocidades
general general
gentleman el caballero
gents los caballeros
German alemán/ana
Germany Alemania
to get obtener/coger
to get up levantarse
gift el regalo
gin la ginebra
girl la niña/la chica
girlfriend la amiga/la novia
to give dar
glad contento/a
glass el vaso
glasses las gafas
glove el guante
to go ir/irse
to go out salir
gold el oro
golf el golf
golf club (group) el club de golf
  (stick) el palo de golf
golf course el campo de golf
good bueno/a
good afternoon las buenas
  tardes
goodbye adiós

good evening las buenas tardes
  /las buenas noches
good morning los buenos días
good night las buenas noches
goods los artículos
government el gobierno
gram el gramo
grandchild el nieto/la nieta
grandfather el abuelo
grandmother la abuela
grandparents los abuelos
grape la uva
grapefruit el pomelo
gravy la salsa
greasy grasiento/a
Greece Grecia
Greek griego/a
green verde
greengrocer's la verdulería
greetings los recuerdos
  /los saludos
grey gris
grill la parrilla
grilled a la parrilla/a la plancha
grocer's la tienda de comestibles
ground el suelo
ground floor la planta baja
group el grupo
guest el/la invitado/a
guest house la casa de
  huéspedes
guide el/la guía
guidebook la guía turística
guided tour la visita
  acompañada
guitar la guitarra

gum (teeth) la encía
  (chewing) el chicle

H
hair el pelo
hairbrush el cepillo para el pelo
hairdresser's la peluquería
hair dryer el secador
hairspray la laca
half la mitad
half board la media pensión
ham el jamón
hamburger la hamburguesa
hammer el martillo
hand la mano
handbag el bolso
handkerchief el pañuelo
handmade hecho/a a mano
hanger la percha
happy feliz
hard duro/a
hard boiled egg el huevo duro
hat el sombrero
to have tener
hay fever la fiebre del heno
head la cabeza
headache el dolor de cabeza
health la salud
heart el corazón
heart attack el ataque
  cardiaco/el infarto
heat el calor
heater el calentador
heating la calefacción
hello! ¡hola!
help! ¡socorro!

help la ayuda
to help ayudar
here aquí
hi-fi el estéreo
high alto/a
high chair la silla para niño
high street la calle principal
to hire alquilar
to hitch-hike hacer autostop
hitch-hiking el autostop
holiday la fiesta
holiday resort el centro
  turístico
holidays las vacaciones
home la casa
home address la dirección
honey la miel
honeymoon la luna de miel
horse el caballo
horse riding montar a caballo
hospital el hospital
hostel el hostal
(youth) hostel el albergue
  juvenil
hot caliente
to be hot (person) tener calor
  (weather) hacer calor
hotel el hotel
hour la hora
house la casa
housewife (la) ama de casa
how? ¿cómo?
how big? ¿De qué tamaño?
how far? ¿A qué distancia?
how long? ¿Cuánto tiempo?
how much? ¿Cuánto?

to be hungry tener hambre
hurry la prisa
to be in a hurry tener prisa
hurry up! ¡de prisa!
to hurt doler
husband el marido

I

ice el hielo
ice cream el helado
ice cube el cubito de hielo
ice rink la pista de hielo
ice skating el patinaje sobre
  hielo
idea la idea
identity card el carnet de
  identidad
ill enfermo/a
illegal ilegal
illness la enfermedad
immediately inmediatamente
to import importar
important importante
impossible imposible
in en
included incluido/a
India la India
Indian indio/a
indigestion la indigestión
indoor el interior
indoor pool la piscina cubierta
industry la industria
infection la infección
infectious contagioso/a
information la información
injection la inyección

injury la herida
inquiries la información
insect bite la picadura de
  insecto
inside dentro (de)
insurance el seguro
(third party) insurance el
  seguro contra terceros
(comprehensive) insurance
  seguro a todo riesgo
insurance company la
  compañía de seguros
interesting interesante
international internacional
interpreter el/la intérprete
intersection el cruce
interval el descanso
to invest invertir
invitation la invitación
to invite invitar
invoice la factura
Ireland Irlanda
Irish irlandés/esa
iron (utensil) la plancha
  (metal) el hierro
to iron planchar
island la isla
Italy Italia
Italian italiano/a
itinerary el itinerario

J

jacket la chaqueta
jail la cárcel
jam la mermelada
jar el tarro

jeans los pantalones vaqueros
jersey el jersey
jewellery las joyas
job el trabajo
juice el jugo/zumo
junction la cruce

K

key la llave
to keep guardar
kind (nice) amable/bueno/a
  (type) el tipo
kitchen la cocina
knee la rodilla
knickers las bragas
knife el cuchillo
to knock (on a door) llamar
to know (facts) saber
  (people) conocer

L

lace (shoe) el cordón
  (fabric) la puntilla
ladder la escalera de mano
ladies (toilets) los servicios de
  señoras
lady la señora
lager la cerveza
lake el lago
lamb el cordero
lamp (table) la lámpara
  (street) el faro
landscape el paisaje
lane (country) el camino
  (motorway) el carril
language el lenguaje/el idioma

  /la lengua
large grande
last último/a
last night anoche
late (time) tarde
  (delayed) retrasado/a
later más tarde
launderette la lavandería
  (automática)
lavatory los servicios
law la ley
lawyer el abogado
laxative el laxante
lead (metal) el plomo
leak la gotera
to leak gotear
lean (meat) magro/sin grasa
to learn aprender
leather el cuero
to leave irse/marcharse/salir
left la izquierda
leg la pierna
leisure el tiempo libre
lemon el limón
lemonade la limonada/la
  gaseosa
lens la lente
  (contact) lente de contacto
lentil la lenteja
less menos
lesson la lección/la clase
letter la carta
lettuce la lechuga
library la biblioteca
licence la licencia/el permiso
  (driving) el carnet de

conducir
to lie down acostarse
lifebelt el cinturón salvavidas
lifeboat el bote salvavidas
lifeguard el/la socorrista
life jacket el chaleco salvavidas
lift el ascensor
light (lamp) la lámpara
  (colour) claro/a
to light encender
light bulb la bombilla
lighter el encendedor
to like gustar
lime la lima
lip el labio
lipstick el lápiz de labios
liqueur el licor
liquid el líquido
to listen oír/escuchar
litre el litro
litter la basura
litter-bin la papelera
little pequeño/a
(a) little un poco
to live vivir
liver el hígado
living room el cuarto de estar
loaf el pan
loaf (long) la barra
lobster la langosta
local local/cercano/a
lock la cerradura
long largo/a
loo el servicio
to look mirar
to look after cuidar

to look for buscar
lorry el camión
to lose perder
lost property los objetos
  perdidos
lounge el salón
love el amor
  (to fall in) love enamorarse
  (end of letter) un abrazo
to love querer
lovely bonito/a
luggage el equipaje
lunch la comida/el almuerzo
lunchtime el mediodía/la hora
  de comer
lung el pulmón

M

machine la máquina
madam la señora
made to measure hecho/a a
  medida
magazine la revista
maid la camarera
mail el correo
main principal
main road la carretera general
to make hacer
make-up el maquillaje
man el hombre
manager el/la director/a
manicure la manicura
many muchos/as
map (road) el mapa
  (town) el plano
margarine la margarina

market el mercado
marmalade la mermelada
married casado/a
mascara el rimel
match (for lighting) la cerilla
  (sport) el partido
material (cloth) la tela
mattress el colchón
maybe quizás
mayonnaise la mayonesa
meal la comida
to mean querer decir
measles el sarampión
to measure medir
measurement la medida
meat la carne
mechanic el/la mecánico
medicine la medicina
to meet encontrar
meeting la reunión
melon el melón
member el socio/la socia
to mend arreglar/reparar
menu el menú
(à la carte) menu la carta
message el recado
meter el contador
metre el metro
midday el mediodía
middle el medio
midnight la medianoche
mild suave
mile la milla
mileage el kilometraje
milk la leche
milk chocolate el chocolate con
  leche
milkshake el batido
mince la carne picada
mineral water (la) agua mineral
minimum mínimo/a
minor menor
minor road la carretera
  secundaria
mint la menta
minute el minuto
miss (title) la señorita
to miss (train) perder
missing desaparecido/a
mistake el error
mistaken equivocado/a
mixed salad la ensalada mixta
mobile phone el teléfono móvil
moisturizing cream la crema
  hidratante
moment el momento
monastery el monasterio
money el dinero
month el mes
more más
morning la mañana
mosquito el mosquito
mosquito bite la picadura de
  mosquito
most la mayoría
mother la madre
motor el motor
motorbike la moto
motorboat la lancha motora
motorist el/la automovilista
motorway la autopista
mountain la montaña

mountain bike la bicicleta de montaña
moustache el bigote
mouth la boca
to move mover
  (house) cambiarse de (casa)
movie la película
Mr señor
Mrs señora
much mucho
mug el tazón
muscle el músculo
museum el museo
mushroom el champiñón
music la música
musical la comedia musical
must (to have to) tener que
mustard la mostaza

N
nail (metal) el clavo
  (finger) la uña
nail polish el esmalte
nail polish remover
  el quitaesmalte (de uñas)
name el nombre
(sur)name el apellido
napkin la servilleta
nappy el pañal
narrow estrecho/a
nationality la nacionalidad
natural natural
near cerca (de)
necessary necesario/a
neck el cuello
necklace el collar

to need necesitar
needle la aguja
neighbour el vecino/la vecina
nephew el sobrino
nervous nervioso/a
never nunca
new nuevo/a
news las noticias
newspaper el periódico
New Zealand Nueva Zelanda
next (in queue) siguiente
  (week etc) próximo/a
next to al lado de
nice (thing) bonito/a
  (person) simpático/a
niece la sobrina
night la noche
nightclub el club/la sala de fiestas
nightdress el camisón
noise el ruido
non-alcoholic (drink) sin alcohol
non-stop (train) directo/a
normal normal
north el norte
Northern Ireland Irlanda del Norte
nose la nariz
nosebleed la hemorragia nasal
note (money) el billete
  (message) el recado
nothing nada
now ahora
nuisance la molestia
number el número
number plate la matrícula

nurse enfermero/a
nut la nuez

O
object el objeto
occupation la profesión
off (food) malo/a
office la oficina
oil el aceite
OK de acuerdo/vale
old viejo/a
olive la oliva/la aceituna
olive oil el aceite de oliva
omelette la tortilla
on sobre/en
one-way (street) la dirección
  única
  (ticket) sencillo
onion la cebolla
only solamente
open abierto/a
to open abrir
open-air al aire libre
opera la ópera
operation la operación
operator el/la telefonista
opposite (place) enfrente (de)
optician óptico/a
or o
orange la naranja
orange juice el zumo de naranja
orangeade la naranjada
orchestra la orquesta
to order pedir
other otro/a
out of order estropeado/a

outside fuera (de)
oven el horno
overdone demasiado hecho/a
overnight por la noche
(to stay) overnight pasar la
  noche
overseas el extranjero
to overtake adelantar
to owe deber
owner el dueño/la dueña

P
package holiday el viaje
  organizado
packet el paquete
paddle boat el patín
pain el dolor
painkiller el calmante
  /el analgésico
painting el cuadro
pair (objects) el par
  (people) la pareja
palace el palacio
panties las bragas
paper el papel
parcel el paquete
pardon? ¿cómo?
parents los padres
park el parque
to park aparcar
parking el aparcamiento
  parking meter el parquímetro
  parking ticket la multa
part la parte
  (car) la pieza
partner (social) el/la

compañero/a
(business) el/la socio/a
party la fiesta
passenger el/la pasajero/a
passport el pasaporte
path el camino
patient el/la paciente
to pay pagar
to pay in (at a bank) ingresar
pea el guisante
peach el melocotón
peanut el cacahuete
pear la pera
pedestrian el/la peatón
pedestrian crossing el paso de
   peatones
peg (clothes) la pinza
pen la pluma
pencil el lápiz
penicillin la penicilina
penis el pene
pensioner el/la pensionista
   /jubilado/a
people la gente
pepper la pimienta
performance
   (theatre) la función
   (cinema) la sesión
perfume el perfume
perhaps quizás
period el periodo
   (menstrual) regla
perm la permanente
permit el permiso
person la persona
petrol la gasolina

petrol pump el surtidor de
   gasolina
petrol station la gasolinera
petrol tank el depósito de
   gasolina
pharmacy la farmacia
phone el teléfono
to phone llamar por teléfono
photo la foto
phrase book el libro de frases
to pick up buscar/recoger
picnic la merienda
picture el cuadro/la imagen
piece el trozo
pig el cerdo
pill la píldora
pillow la almohada
pin el alfiler
pineapple la piña
pink rosa
pipe (water) la tubería
   (tobacco) la pipa
place el lugar
plan el plan
   (map) el plano
plane el avión
plant la planta
plastic el plástico
plate el plato
platform el andén/la vía
play (theatre) la obra
to play (game) jugar
   (instrument) tocar
playground zona de juegos
   infantiles
pleasant agradable

please por favor
plug (sink) el tapón
  (electrical) el enchufe
to plug in enchufar
plum la ciruela
plumber el/la fontanero/a
pocket el bolsillo
police la policía
policeman el policía
policewoman la mujer policía
pool (swimming) la piscina
poor pobre
popular popular
port (harbour) el puerto
  (drink) el vino de Oporto
pork el cerdo
porter (attendant) el mozo
  (doorman) el portero
portion la porción
Portugal Portugal
Portuguese portugués/esa
possible posible
post el correo
to post enviar/mandar/echar
postage stamp el sello
post box la buzón
postcard la tarjeta postal
post code el código postal
post man el cartero
poster el cartel
post office la oficina de
  correos
potato la patata
pottery (objects) la cerámica
powder el polvo
pram el cochecito de niño

prawn la gamba
precaution la precaución
to prefer preferir
pregnant embarazada
to prepare preparar
prescription la receta
present (gift) el regalo
press (newspapers) la prensa
to press (button) empujar
to press (trousers) planchar
pretty bonito/a
price el precio
private
  (personal) privado/a/
  personal
  (lesson etc) particular
prize el premio
probably probablemente
problem el problema
profession la profesión
programme el programa
prohibited prohibido/a
property la propiedad
proprietor el/la propietario/a/
  dueño/a
to prosecute proseguir
to protect proteger
pub la taberna/el pub
public el público
public transport el servicio de
  transportes públicos
to pull tirar
pullover el jersey
punch (drink) el ponche
  (blow) el golpe
puncture el pinchazo

purse el monedero
to push empujar
to put poner
pyjamas el pijama

Q

quality la calidad
quantity la cantidad
quarter el cuarto
queasy mareado/a
question la pregunta
queue la cola
to queue hacer cola
quick rápido/a
quickly rápidamente
quiet silencioso/a

R

rabbit el conejo
race (sport) la carrera
racket la raqueta
radiator el radiador
radio la radio
railway el ferrocarril
rain la lluvia
to rain llover
raincoat el impermeable
rape la violación
to rape violar
rare (meat) poco/a hecho/a
  (unusual) raro/a
rash la erupción/el sarpullido
raspberry la frambuesa
raw (uncooked) crudo/a
razor la navaja

(safety) razor la maquinilla
  de afeitar
(electric) razor la máquina de
  afeitar eléctrica
razor blade la hoja de afeitar
to reach (arrive at) llegar
to read leer
ready preparado/a/listo/a
real real/verdadero/a
receipt el recibo/el ticket
receive recibir
recent reciente
reception (hotel) la recepción
receptionist el/la recepcionista
to recommend recomendar
record (music) el disco
recorded delivery el certificado
record-player el estéreo
to recover recuperar (se)
red rojo/a
refrigerator el frigorífico
  /la nevera
refund el reembolso
to refuse negar
regular regular
relative (family) el/la
  pariente/a
to relax relajar/descansar
to remain quedarse
to remember
  recordar/acordarse
to remove sacar/quitar
rent el alquiler
to rent alquilar
to repair reparar/arreglar
to repeat repetir

to replace sustituir
to represent representar
representative el/la representante
request la demanda
to request pedir
to reserve reservar
resort el centro turístico
responsible responsable
rest el descanso
to rest descansar
restaurant el restaurante
result el resultado
retired (person) el/la jubilado/a
return (ticket) un billete de ida y vuelta
to return (go back) volver
(money) devolver
reverse (gear) la marcha atrás
rib la costilla
rice el arroz
rich rico/a
to ride (a horse) montar (a caballo)
right (direction) la derecha
to be right tener razón
rights los derechos
ring (jewellery) el anillo
to ring (phone) llamar
(bell) sonar
ring road la carretera de circunvalación
rink la pista
ripe maduro/a
risk el riesgo

river el río
road el camino/la carretera
road sign la señal de tráfico
roadworks las obras
roast asado/a
to rob robar
roll (bread) el panecillo
roof el tejado
roof rack la baca
room (house) el cuarto
(hotel) la habitación
rope la cuerda
round redondo/a
route la ruta
row (theatre) la fila
rubbish la basura
rucksack la mochila
rude grosero/a
ruins las ruinas
rules el reglamento
to run correr

S
sad triste
safe (for money) la caja fuerte
(no danger) seguro/a
safety pin el imperdible
to sail navegar
sailing boat el velero
salad la ensalada
salad cream la mayonesa
salad dressing la vinagreta
salami el salchichón
sale la venta/las rebajas
(for) sale se vende
salesperson dependiente/a

salmon el salmón
salt la sal
sand la arena
sandal la sandalia
sandwich el sandwich
  /el bocadillo
sanitary towel la compresa
sardine la sardina
sauce la salsa
saucepan la cacerola
saucer el platito
sausage la salchicha
scarf el pañuelo
  (woollen) la bufanda
scenery el paisaje
school la escuela
scissors las tijeras
Scotland Escocia
Scottish escocés/esa
screwdriver el destornillador
sea el/la mar
seafood los mariscos
sea front el paseo marítimo
seaside la costa
season la temporada
seasoning el condimento
season ticket el abono
seat el asiento
seat belt el cinturón de
  seguridad
second segundo/a
secretary el/la secretario/a
section la sección
to see ver
see you later! ¡hasta luego!
self-service el autoservicio

to sell vender
to send enviar
to serve servir
service el servicio
serviette la servilleta
to sew coser
shade la sombra
shampoo el champú
sharp agudo/a
to shave afeitarse
shaver la maquinilla de afeitar
shaving cream la crema de
  afeitar
sheet (bed) la sábana
  (of paper) la hoja
shellfish los mariscos
sherry el jerez
ship el barco
shirt la camisa
shoe el zapato
shoelace el cordón de zapatos
shoe repairer's el/la
  zapatero/a
shoe shop la zapatería
shop la tienda
shop assistant el/la
  dependiente/a
shopping las compras
(to go) shopping ir de compras
shopping centre el centro
  comercial
short corto/a
shorts los pantalones cortos
short-sighted miope
show el espectáculo
to show mostrar

shower la ducha
shut cerrado/a
sick (ill) enfermo/a
  (sea/air) mareado/a
sickness la enfermedad
side effects los efectos
  secundarios
sightseeing la visita turística
sign la señal
to sign firmar
signature la firma
silk la seda
silly tonto/a
silver la plata
since desde
singer el/la cantante
single (bed, room) individual
  (person) el/la soltero/a
single ticket un billete
  sencillo/de ida
sink (bathroom) el lavabo
sir señor
sister la hermana
size (clothes) la talla
  (shoes) el número
  (object) el tamaño
to skate patinar
skating el patinaje
skating rink la pista de patinaje
ski el esquí
to ski esquiar
ski lift el telesquí/la telesilla
skin la piel
skirt la falda
to sleep dormir
sleeping bag el saco de dormir

sleeping car el coche cama
slide (photo) la diapositiva
slipper la zapatilla
slow despacio/lento/a
small pequeño/a
small change el dinero suelto
to smoke fumar
smoker fumador/a
snack la tapa
snack bar la cafetería
snow la nieve
soap el jabón
socks los calcetines
soft (bed) blando/a
  (texture) suave
sole (shoe) la suela
  (fish) el lenguado
some unos/as
someone alguien
something algo
sometimes a veces
son el hijo
soon pronto
sore doloroso/a
sore throat el dolor de garganta
sorry! ¡perdón!/¡lo siento!
soup la sopa
south el sur
South Africa Sudáfrica
South African sudafricano/a
South America Sudamérica
South American
  sudamericano/a
souvenirs los regalos
spade la pala
Spain España

Spanish español/a
spanner la llave inglesa
spare part el recambio
spare tyre la rueda de repuesto
spark-plug la bujía
to speak hablar
special especial
speciality la especialidad
speed la velocidad
speed limit la velocidad máxima
to spell escribir/deletrear
to spend gastar
spicy picante
spinach la espinaca
spine la espina dorsal
splinter la astilla
sponge la esponja
  (cake) el bizcocho
spoon la cuchara
sport el deporte
spot (medical) el grano
  (place) el sitio
to sprain torcer
spring la primavera
square (shape) cuadrado/a
  (in a town) la plaza
stadium el estadio
staff el personal
stain la mancha
stain remover el quitamanchas
stairs las escaleras
stall (market) el puesto
  (theatre) la butaca/el patio
  de butacas
stamp el sello
to start empezar

  (car) arrancar
starter el motor de arranque
station la estación
stationer's la papelería
to stay quedarse/alojarse
steak el bistec
to steal robar
steering-wheel el volante
sterling la libra esterlina
sticking plaster la tirita
stiff neck la tortícolis
sting la picadura
stockings las medias
stomach el estómago
stop (bus) la parada
to stop parar
store (small) la tienda
  (large) los almacenes
straight recto/a
straight ahead todo recto
straight away en seguida
straw la paja
strawberry la fresa
street la calle
student el/la estudiante
subtitled subtitulado/a/con
  subtítulos
suede el ante
sugar el azúcar
suit el traje
suitable apto/a
suitcase la maleta
summer el verano
sun el sol
to sunbathe tomar el sol
sunburn la quemadura de sol

sunglasses las gafas de sol
sunshade la sombrilla
sunstroke la insolación
sun-tan lotion el bronceador
supermarket el supermercado
supper la cena
supplement el suplemento
suppository el supositorio
sure seguro/a
surgery (doctor's) el consultorio
  (operation) la cirugía
surname el apellido
sweater el suéter
sweet dulce
  (dessert) el postre
sweets los caramelos
sweetcorn el maíz
sweetener el edulcorante
sweetshop la confitería
to swell hinchar
to swim nadar
swimming la natación
swimming costume el traje de
  baño
swimming pool la piscina
swimming trunks el bañador de
  caballero
switch el interruptor
to switch on encender
to switch off apagar
swollen hinchado/a
symptom el síntoma
syrup (medicine) el jarabe
  (fruit) el almíbar

T
table la mesa
table-cloth el mantel
to take llevar/tomar
talc los polvos de talco
tall alto/a
tampon el tampón
tap el grifo
tape la cinta
tart la tarta
tax el impuesto
tax free libre de impuestos
taxi el taxi
taxi rank la parada de taxis
tea el té
teacher el/la profesor/a
teaspoon la cucharilla
tea towel el trapo de cocina
telephone el teléfono
telephone box la cabina
  telefónica
telephone directory la guía
  telefónica
television la televisión
  (set) el televisor
to tell decir
temperature la temperatura
  (fever) la fiebre
tennis el tenis
tennis court la pista de tenis
tent la tienda de campaña
terrace la terraza
test el examen
  (medical) el análisis
to text mandar un mensaje (al
  móvil)

thank you gracias

that ése/ésa

theft el robo

then entonces

there allí

thermometer el termómetro

thick grueso/a

thief el ladrón/la ladrona

thin delgado/a

thing la cosa

to think pensar

  (to believe) creer

to be thirsty tener sed

this el éste/la ésta

those los ésos/las ésas

thousand mil

thread el hilo

throat la garganta

through a través

  no through road la calle sin
  salida

ticket (train/bus) el billete

  (cinema) la entrada

  (shopping) el recibo

  (parking) la multa

ticket office la taquilla

tide la marea

tie la corbata

tights los pantis/los leotardos

time (clock) la hora

  (general) el tiempo

timetable el horario

tin (can) la lata

tin-opener el abrelatas

tip (money) la propina

tired cansado/a

tissue (handkerchief) el
  pañuelo de papel

to a/hacia

toast la tostada

tobacco el tabaco

tobacconist's el estanco

today hoy

toe el dedo del pie

together juntos/as

toilet el servicio

toilet paper el papel higiénico

toll el peaje

tomato el tomate

tomorrow mañana

tonic water la tónica

tonight esta noche

tooth el diente

toothache el dolor de muelas

toothbrush el cepillo de dientes

toothpaste la pasta de dientes

toothpick el palillo

torch la linterna

total total

tour la excursión

tourist office la oficina de
  turismo

towel la toalla

town la ciudad

  (small) el pueblo

town hall el ayuntamiento

toy el juguete

tracksuit el chándal

traffic el tráfico

traffic light el semáforo

traffic warden el/la guardia de
  tráfico

train el tren
transfer (bank) la transferencia
to translate traducir
translator el/la traductor/a
to transport transportar
travel el viaje
travel agency la agencia de viajes
traveller's cheque el cheque de viaje
tree el árbol
trolley el carrito
trousers los pantalones
to try (food) probar
T-shirt la camiseta
tuna el atún
Turkey Turquía
turkey el pavo
Turkish turco/a
turn (in road) la curva
to turn (a corner) doblar
twice las dos veces
twist (ankle) torcer (tobillo)
type la clase
typical típico/a
tyre el neumático/la rueda

U

ugly feo/a
umbrella el paraguas
uncomfortable incómodo/a
unconscious inconsciente
uncooked crudo/a
under debajo (de)
underdone (meat) poco hecho/a
underground (train) el metro

underpants los calzoncillos
to understand comprender
underwear la ropa interior
United States Estados Unidos
unleaded sin plomo
until hasta
up arriba
upset (angry) enfadado/a
upstairs arriba
urgent urgente
to use usar
useful útil

V

vacancy la habitación libre
vacation las vacaciones
vaccine la vacuna
vacuum cleaner la aspiradora
valley el valle
value el valor
valuables los objetos de valor
van la furgoneta
veal la ternera
vegetable la verdura
vegetarian vegetariano/a
velvet el terciopelo
very muy
vest la camiseta
video machine el vídeo
video tape la cinta de vídeo
view la vista
villa el chalet
village el pueblo
vinegar el vinagre
visa el visado
visit la visita

to visit visitar
vodka el/la vodka
voice la voz
voltage el voltaje
to vomit vomitar

W

to wait esperar
waiter el camarero
waiting-room la sala de espera
waitress la camarera
to wake (up) despertar(se)
Wales Gales
walk el paseo
to walk andar
wall la pared
wallet la cartera
walnut la nuez
to want querer
ward (hospital) la sala
wardrobe el armario
to wash lavar
to wash the dishes fregar los
  platos
washable lavable
wash-basin el lavabo
washing machine la lavadora
washing powder el detergente
washing-up liquid el lavavajillas
wasp la avispa
watch el reloj
watch strap la correa de reloj
water (la) agua
watermelon la sandía
water-skiing el esquí acuático
watt el vatio

weak débil
weather el tiempo
weather forecast el boletín
  meteorológico
wedding la boda
week la semana
weekday el día laborable
weekend el fin de semana
to weigh pesar
weight el peso
welcome bienvenido/a
well bien
well done bien hecho/a
Welsh galés/esa
west el oeste
wet mojado/a
what qué/cómo
where dónde
which cuál/qué
while mientras
white blanco/a
who quién
why por qué
wide ancho/a
wife la mujer/la esposa
to win ganar
wind el viento
window la ventana
(shop) window el escaparate
windscreen el parabrisas
windscreen wiper
  el limpiaparabrisas
wine el vino
winter el invierno
with con
without sin

witness el/la testigo
woman la mujer
wood (material) la madera
  (forest) el bosque
wool la lana
word la palabra
work el trabajo
to work (person) trabajar
  (machine) funcionar
work permit el permiso de
  trabajo
world el mundo
to worry preocuparse
  don't worry! ¡no se preocupe!
wound la herida
to wrap envolver
wrapping paper el papel de
  envolver
wrist la muñeca
to write escribir
writing paper el papel de carta
wrong (mistaken)
  equivocado/a

X
X-ray (department) la
  radiografía
X-rays los rayos X (equis)

Y
yacht el yate
year el año
yellow amarillo/a
yes sí
yesterday ayer
yet aún

(already) ya
yoghurt el yogur
you (informal) tú
  (formal) usted
young joven
youth hostel el albergue juvenil